THEOLOGICAL EXPLORATIONS

THEOLOGICAL EXPLORATIONS

Paul M. van Buren

The Macmillan Company · New York

Collier-Macmillan Limited · London

Acknowledgment is made for permission to reprint the following:

"Theology in the Context of Culture" from the series "How I am Making Up My Mind," *The Christian Century*, April 7, 1965, Copyright 1965 by Christian Century Foundation, reprinted in *Frontline Theology*, edited by Dean Peerman, © M. E. Bratcher, 1967 (Richmond, Virginia: John Knox Press); "The Dissolution of the Absolute," *Religion in Life*, Summer 1965 (Nashville, Tennessee: The Abingdon Press); "Christian Education Post Mortem Dei," *Religious Education*, January-February, 1965 (New York: The Religious Education Association); "Bonhoeffer's Paradox: Living with God without God," *Union Seminary Quarterly Review*, Fall, 1967, Copyright © 1967 by Union Theological Seminary in the City of New York, reprinted in *Bonhoeffer in a World Come of Age* (Philadelphia: Fortress Press, 1968); "William James and Metaphysical Risk," part of a forthcoming book entitled *American Philosophy and the Future*, edited by Michael Novak to be published by Charles Scribner's Sons in 1968 and used by special permission of Charles Scribner's Sons and Curtis Brown, Ltd.; and "Interlude" from *Homage to Clio*, W. H. Auden, © Copyright 1960 by W. H. Auden (New York: Random House, Inc. and London: Faber & Faber, Ltd.).

Library of Congress Catalog Card Number: 68-16766

FIRST PRINTING

The Macmillan Company, New York
Collier-Macmillan Canada Ltd., Toronto, Ontario

Printed in the United States of America

Contents

INTRODUCTION   1

I   How I Am: Making Up My Mind   15

II   The Dissolution of the Absolute   27

III   What Do We Mean by "An Empirical Investigation of the Church"?   43

IV   Christian Education in a Pragmatic Age   61

V   On Doing Theology   79

VI   Bonhoeffer's Paradox: Living With God Without God   107

VII   William James and Metaphysical Risk   133

VIII   Is Transcendence the Word We Want?   161

Introduction:
On Theological Explorations

"THEOLOGICAL EXPLORATIONS" IS A TITLE WHICH MIGHT be taken in more ways than one. There was a time, not long past, in which it would have been taken, probably unambiguously, to mean the exploration of territory unmapped by theologians, exploration setting out from the well-established base camp of theological doctrine and equipped with accepted and tested theological method. So conceived, the theological explorer would set out to map and hopefully plant the cross on foreign shores. He would have been said by some to have been engaged in the task of "making theology relevant" to this or that element in human thought or activity, be it in the arts or sciences. Theology, with its point of departure and its modus operandi, would have been assumed to be given; it was the new land which had to be explored.

The essays in this volume are of another sort. What is being explored here is theology itself. The question lying behind each of these essays is this: if there is a human activity in our time which we may call theology, of what sort is it? What is the character of the theological enterprise in our present situation? The old base camp and the time-tested old equipment is just what is in question here. Theological explorations, according to this model, are hypothetical investigations in which now one, now another site for departure is tried out, it being not yet settled whether it shall prove a camp to return to and enlarge as a base for future explorations, or shall be left behind as a campsite not to be used again.

The equipment is also tentative and one function of

these explorations is to test out old and new methods in order to see how far and with what results now this, now that way of doing theology will take one. The terrain to be explored is, I suppose, no better understood than it was in the older model, but now the focus of our questions is the nature of the theological enterprise itself, what it is that the believer is doing with the words he uses, what he is saying about himself, human life and the world.

Since these essays are the explorations of one person, they have certain common features. It will be evident, I think, that I am trying out a particular method, or variations on a particular method. Since completing *The Secular Meaning of the Gospel,* I have been engaged in a sustained conversation with Wittgenstein's *Philosophical Investigations,* a book which fascinates and puzzles me more and in ever new ways each time I work through it. Language and what we do with words has consequently been my preoccupation. The voice of John Wisdom has also made itself heard in this conversation, and in recent years William James has increasingly taken part. Taken together, these influences should give some idea of what it would mean to say that the way of doing theology which is being explored here is linguistic and empirical, pragmatic and pluralistic, and that increasingly the metaphysical character of theology is being explored.

I do not argue that the lines of thought suggested by the names of Wittgenstein and Wisdom on the one hand and William James on the other are the only fruitful ones to pursue in carrying out theological explorations today. I would prefer to say that these are the voices which come through more clearly and hauntingly to me than do those of others—e.g., Heidegger, French existentialists, and Whitehead. Others may explore these other lines, but I think that in sticking to the linquistic and pragmatic thinkers of our time I am listening to voices in our contemporary culture which theology today can ignore only to its own loss. William James particularly strikes me as a thinker worth far more attention than he has received, and not only from theologians.

The essays which follow cover a period of just four years. They are not placed in chronological order, as the development, if any, is not of a chronological sort. Not one of these essays represents my "position," past or present, except in the way that one frame of a moving picture film represents the "position" of the dancer it portrays. What may interest us in a dancer is the movement of the dance itself, rather than a momentary frozen "position," and what we look for in the way of development is a certain "loosening up" or grace in the way the dancer performs. I like to think that at least in some of these essays I have overcome in part a certain "muscle-bound" quality of my last book, but gracefulness, like grace, is not won by effort and its presence is best judged by the careful observer.

Turning from the exploratory character of these essays to the other side of the title, in what sense are these essays theological? The answer may be given in a rather traditional form: they are concerned directly or indirectly and in their own way with man's language about God. Now that the hot air has leaked out of the recent "death of God" balloon, and as we push the flaccid remains to the back of the drawer reserved for mementos of our more foolish exploits, it may be said that behind all that journalistic nonsense lay an important issue. It is an old issue in a contemporary form: a rediscovery in our time that man's question about God, or about the meaning of life, or however it may be put, does not long admit of clear and simple answers. Indeed, it would seem that it gains its importance in human life in its role as a question, rather than from any of the particular answers which men have given to it. Among all the other characteristics of man, he is also the creature who, at least in some cases or on some occasions, asks the religious question, in one way or another.

So fascinating are some of the answers which have been made to the question about God or the meaning of life, that it is easy to concentrate our attention on these answers. In one view of the matter, that is what theology is about: getting clear about the answer. In the course of time, however, any answer, once made at all clear, seems to prove unsatisfactory, and the clearer is the answer worked out by one generation, the more uncomfortable with it becomes the next generation. Something of this sort, in any case, would appear to have happened in recent times, the answer of "Neo-Orthodoxy" of the nineteen-twenties and thirties having become an orthodoxy of the forties and fifties which became increasingly inadequate in the sixties.

If there is any validity to this analysis, it would seem wise not to rush on so rapidly over the question to look for an answer, but rather to linger and reflect more carefully on the question itself, on man as one who asks this question, and on the occasions on which or the form of life in which men speak of God. Theologians and religionists are not, of course, the only ones who pass too quickly over the question. There are also those, possibly the great majority of men today, who simply ignore the question, dismiss it, or even argue that it is illegitimate. The only questions men ask that are worth pursuing, for many today, are those which admit of clear answers. This attitude is part of what we have in mind when we use the word "secular" in a pejorative sense. It should be noted, however, that the superficial secularist is doing only what the orthodox theologian does in his way, rushing on to get clear about the answer, viewing man as the problem-solver, not the problem-poser.

Two essays in the analysis of religious discourse illustrate the issue, both published in the paperback *The Existence of God,* edited by John Hick: R. B. Braithwaite's "An Empiricist View of the Nature of Religious Belief," and John Wisdom's "The Modes of Thought and the Logic of God." A comparison of the procedure of the two authors reveals the difference resulting from approaching the subject in opposite ways. Braithwaite begins by testing whether religious statements fall into the three classes

7

of those statements "whose method of truth-value testing is in general outline clear." Clarity is his aim, and clarity is the only criterion he gives for beginning with statements about particular empirical facts, scientific hypotheses, and the propositions of logic and mathematics. It should not be surprising that he does not find religious statements to fit any of these classes, but it ill behooves religionists to flee from his finding—that religious statements, like moral statements, are declarations of an intention to behave in a certain way—in order to attempt to establish religious statements in one of the specified and "clear" classes. What is of interest, however, beyond his suggestion that more attention needs to be paid to "the part played by imagination in religion," a suggestion which, if followed, would pose serious questions about the structure of Braithwaite's whole fascinating argument, is the fact that religious statements become, in this treatment, just as clear as the classes with which Braithwaite began, as clear and as flat. If one is left with a sense that this interesting argument has not done justice to the subject, the fault may be assigned to the point of departure rather than to the resultant analysis of the function of religious language. If one wishes above all else to be factual and clear, one will hunt far to find a better answer than that provided by Braithwaite to the question of what religion is.

John Wisdom's essay, on the other hand, is far less clear and provides no neat answer. In a haunting, provocative and thoughtful way, he rambles around the theme of language which is unclear, beginning and ending with the comment of the friend of a woman trying on a hat, "My dear, it's the Taj Mahal." Every attempt to translate that wild assertion into something more sensible—and flat— such as, "It is in some respects like the Taj Mahal," is resisted as leading only to the "negligible stuff that so often results from trying to put poetry into prose." Poetry into prose! Clever, careful, clear, and in its way correct as Braithwaite's essay is, surely Wisdom has come closer to the heart of the matter. Wisdom is asking us not to discuss or treat lightly "a move in thought which from a mass of data . . . builds up into the proof of something which, though it doesn't go beyond that data, gives us an apprehension of reality which before we lacked." Such can poetry be. Is religion of this sort? Be that as it may, Wisdom's starting point is just the opposite of Braithwaite's, in the realm of the poetic, the metaphor which cannot well be reduced to a set of similes. No less critical attention is needed here, no less need for all possible clarity is allowed, Wisdom concludes, but the point of departure which determines the comparison used in our reflections on the function and character of religious discourse are clearly of prime importance if we are not to overlook the features of religious discourse which make it what it is. If Wisdom gives us a less finished picture than Braithwaite, he leaves the reader more sure that he has not overlooked that for which he was hunting.

If we stop to reflect on the questions which man poses to himself, the most intriguing are those without clear or easy answers. Such are his questions about himself, his life, and his God. They are, perhaps, all the same question, and on the hypothesis that they are, doing theology is the exploration of such questions and of man as the one who raises such questions. One could call such explorations humanistic. One could call them philosophical. One may also call them theological.

To call such investigations theological suggests that the questions are considered as posed in a certain context. The context would be Western rather than Eastern, for example, and probably the Christian tradition in the West, or the remains and strains of that tradition. I am not quite sure what it would mean to say that these questions raised in this context today are the same as (or different from) the major questions about life and the self as they have been or are raised in other contexts and cultures. Without prejudice to other ways in which man has found himself and his world a source of wonder to himself, the essays that follow are theological in the sense that they are directed to the religious question in the Western tradition as it is raised for at least some in the English-speaking world today.

A few words of introduction to the particular essays may help to orient the reader. I do not want to impose an order or systematic development on them, for that would imply that I have been exploring with the aim of finding theology. In fact it seems evident to me at this time that exploration itself is the proper mode and character of theology for our time. Moreover, each of these essays is occasional in the sense that each was written in response to a specific invitation or request. The subjects were given, although what I chose to do with them was in each case my own responsibility. On both counts, therefore, it would be inappropriate to look for a system underlying these essays.

The first chapter is the original form—and title—of an article written early in 1965 for *The Christian Century* as part of their "How-I-Am-Making-Up-My-Mind" series. It can serve as a general introduction to the others. The second chapter was written in 1965 for a symposium published in *Religion in Life* around the subject "The Values and Dangers of the Present Secular Emphasis." The essay is one attempt to make clear the features of our context which I find unavoidable in exploring the character of a contemporary theology.

The third chapter is an unpublished paper prepared for a Faith and Order Study Commission in 1963. This commission was given the assignment of sorting out a problem defined (?) as "Order and Organization," and we found ourselves soon involved in the problem of the relationship between "theological" and "sociological" views of the church. This paper was prepared in connection with our discussions as an attempt to sort out the problem of apparently conflicting languages, and especially to clarify what might be meant by speaking of an empirical study of the church. I need hardly say that this paper was my own and did not represent the common mind of that Study Commission.

Chapter Four was written in 1964 as the lead article in a symposium published in *Religious Education,* which included eight different responses to my article and a brief reply from me. In this essay I began to explore, very briefly, the metaphysical status of theology, but the main idea explored is to what extent religious faith revolves about the telling of the religious story. I have made a few minor changes in wording in the title and text to avoid misunderstandings.

Chapter Five, not previously published, was written in 1964 as one of the four papers for the colloquium held at Drew University on the theme "The Problem of Non-objectifying Thinking and Speaking in Contemporary Theology." Heinrich Ott's paper, which serves as a sort of foil for sections of the chapter, may be found in *The Later Heidegger and Theology.*[1] The colloquium theme and the work of many of the participants represented a way of doing theology that was foreign to me, and this essay was my attempt to show by contrast some of the advantages, as I saw it, of doing theology in conversation with analytic rather than Heideggerian philosophy.

Chapters Six and Seven were both written in 1967 and represent two parts of another exploration, this time taking William James as a companion, even at times as a guide. The first was written for a symposium on Bonhoeffer held at Union Theological Seminary and to be published before this is in print in *The Union Seminary Quarterly Review* and also by Fortress Press. The second was written for a forthcoming volume on the future of

American philosophy being edited by Michael Novak and to be published by Scribners. The last chapter was written in 1965 as a contribution to a volume on radical theology being edited by Gabriel Vahanian.

Insofar as theology takes the form of exploration, it lives off of conversation, and I wish to dedicate this volume to my students and colleagues of the Department of Religion of Temple University, who in their openness, diversity, and quality provide such a fruitful context in which to carry on the work of theological explorations. The unfinished, even conflicting elements in some of these explorations and the contradictions between some of the results is a sign that the conversation is far from finished and still has a long way to go.

NOTES

[1] *The Later Heidegger and Theology,* J. M. Robinson and J. B. Cobb, Jr., eds. (New York: Harper & Row, 1963).

I

How I Am:
Making Up My Mind

GETTING THERE IS HALF THE FUN, THE SAYING GOES, BUT I am inclined to think that in theology in this generation, getting there can and had better be all the fun. The title of this series and at least some of the contributions to it might give the impression that some specifiable destination lies ahead and that making up one's mind is to be done with a view to that goal. My emended punctuation in the title of this article is intended to suggest a way of doing theology without such a goal, without even knowing what it would be to "arrive." I find myself today, and I fully expect to spend my life, making up my mind.

The last time I had business with *The Christian Century,* my contribution was considered so inappropriate, apparently, that I was editorially classified as "a philosopher," as a justification for asking "a theologian" to write another article on the same subject. I am sure it must be difficult for this journal to bear such a title in such a century and I readily forgive the editors for their nervousness, but, for the sake of the record, I must say that I found that classification amusing. I am, have been all along, and undoubtedly (in my own way) shall go on making up my mind as a theologian. Philosophy is a good game, too, of course, but it is not really my game. I find it invigorating exercise and especially helpful for one brought up to regard philosophy as something best avoided by theologians. I have even felt that a certain respect for words and the workings of our language is important for getting clear about a number of puzzles. But the puzzles on which I work are related in one way or another to the religious or theological game. If some in that game dislike the way I play it or think that I am in the wrong court, I can only say it is still the game I am trying to play, though I admit that as time goes on I find myself losing interest in getting all the labels on just right.

In this connection I would say that it has become increasingly clear to me that you have to pay a price to get into that stadium in which a variety of language games is played. Linguistic analysis has become something of a fad among theologians during the past few years and I have given up trying to keep up with all the writing on the subject of so-called religious language, but I have the impression that few seem to appreciate the fact that you have to pay for a ticket to get into the language-games stadium. The price, I believe, would be considered steep by quite a few who seem to have wandered in without paying. My guess is that the gate-crashers will have to pay up eventually or else go home.

Due to peculiarities or perhaps deficiencies in my education or character, it has been my fate to discover many things backward. I discovered Schleiermacher, Feuerbach, and Nietzsche, for example, only long after I had discovered Barth. I also figured out what logical positivism was up to only after I had discovered Wittgenstein's *Philosophical Investigations*. Whatever the obvious disavantages of this fact, it does mean that I never found myself hemmed in by A. J. Ayer and his verification principle, gasping for theological air. Consequently, I did not discover Wittgenstein as a great release from *that* problem. Many who seem to have greeted linguistic analysis with shouts of joy have done so, so they imply, because it made it possible for them to say that among all the variety of language games, there could now be also a religious language game.

If movement out of the two-game world of positivism, where only analytic and synthetic (or empirical) games were allowed, into a stadium in which a multiplicity of games was recognized was a great release, surely the price of the metaphysics of this stadium had to be paid: in the world of language *games*, there could be no one game that was *the* game. Wittgenstein's game theory works, if it works at all, in a pluralistic and relativistic world, and if one cannot or will not accept that world, one had better not play in that stadium. Exploration of the variety of language games is an exploration of the variety of forms of life, with all the joys and pains and mysteries of a world of multiplicity and relativity.

One of the ways in which I am going about making up my mind is by putting myself in what is for me a new context: a department of religion in the liberal arts college of a large, secular, urban university. This recent change of context, after seven years in a denominational theological school, has come about through my concern to explore the role and function of theology in a wider context than that offered by even a remarkably open and permissive ecclesiastical institution. I hasten to add that I would probably not be where I now find myself had it not been for the particular group of colleagues with whom I worked at that institution and our common concern to reflect on the theological question as it arises in our particular society. Nevertheless, the questions which one asks oneself or is able to hear, and the way in which one goes about trying to answer them, are—or have been for me—partly determined by the context in which one works. The change of context which I have chosen reflects my concern to ask and hear more clearly the religious question as it arises in our society, rather than as it arises in a professional ecclesiastical context. I am not sure what it would mean to say that this is a better or a worse way to go about doing theology. I do think, however, that it is a different way, and, although I have been at it too short a time to see the scope of that difference, some of its features may be suggested.

In making up my mind about the function, content, and norms of theology, I find myself reflecting increasingly on the function, content, and norms of religion in its cultural context, and more specifically, upon the contemporary form of the question. Three years ago, when I was finishing *The Secular Meaning of the Gospel*, I was moving in this direction after a number of years of wrestling with the problems of classical Christology within the context of the church. That book represented an important step in a personal struggle to overcome my own theological past. It served to help me over a hump. Having found myself on the other side, I have been occupied since then with finding my way about in the realm outside a "theological circle" which was becoming increasingly unreal. I am trying to see the role and nature of theology in the context of the plurality and relativity of contemporary culture. The breadth of and diversity within this context makes this an untidy task, but I find I must work away at it in order to win more clarity about where I am as I go about making up my mind, or about what sort of mind it is that I am trying to "make up," and in what "making up" such a mind in such a time and place consists. Such a project is never finished, of course, and must by the nature of the case be fragmentary and tentative, but I find I must keep at this for myself, regardless of whether the results turn out to be of interest to anyone else.

Exploring religious thought or theology in its cultural rather than in its ecclesiastical context is partly an exercise in the employment of models. So thoroughly was I brought up theologically to see the nineteenth century as a theological catastrophe, leading to a "dead end" until the renaissance of the twenties and thirties of this century, that it has taken me a long time to break away from the captivity of that image. I now want to try a musical model, with religious thought conceived as part of the accompaniment to melody carried by the life and thought in our culture. With this perspective, the course of theology from the nineteenth into the twentieth century might not appear to be on the road to oblivion at all. Instead, the second quarter of this century might be thought of as an era in which theology refused to continue the concert and went off into a corner to practice a more ancient melody.

The present task, then, would be to go back, pick up the score as it was being played some decades back, and see if we can catch up with the way in which the main melody has been developing, changing key, even changing tonal structure, with the hope of adding an accompaniment which might help round out a score that seems at times to be a bit hollow. It may even be that important dissonances might be created which could help lead to the resolution of some painful discords in the present score.

What I have in mind here is a model, not a description. The task of testing this model, of going over the material and seeing how it looks when viewed in this way, is a large order and will take a good deal of time. Undoubtedly the model will have to be recast again and again as this work proceeds, but if there is any merit in it, it may serve to make it more possible to see more clearly than I do at this point just what the role of faith and theology might be in the world of technology and revolutionary change into which we have just begun to move. Getting clear about the way in which our American society has been changing over the past hundred years is itself an almost endless task, but until some understanding of this is achieved, it would make little sense to try to "get with it" and begin the work of doing theology as a constructive and critical contribution to human thought.

Theology has been traditionally a discipline in the service of the church, but the church today does not seem to be a community, much less one with a clear identity.

Theology has been grounded in the Bible, but the Bible is apparently little read and less understood. Theology has operated with a monistic cosmology and metaphysics which seems to have little or no relationship to our culture and its way of seeing how things are in this society. So-called Neo-Orthodoxy or Biblical Theology (both are rough and most inexact labels) has been a damper which has hindered us from moving with the times and finding new ways in which to conceive the task of theology. Such at the moment are the ideas with which I am occupied as I go on with the business of making up my mind.

What might theology be in the cultural context in which we now live? To this question I can give only the most tentative sort of answer at this time, but I am forced by my situation to do at least that, for I teach and study in a department of religion set up within a college of liberal arts. The *raison d'être* of this department, insofar as I understand the situation, lies in the thesis that the study of man's religious ideas is a part of the whole study of man. Religious studies form a piece of the humanities. If we wish to understand human life in the fullness of its development and scope, we must look at man's religious thought and practice, as well as at his history, literature and philosophy, his politics and economics, his scientific and technological accomplishments. Whether it is good that religion has played an important part in human life is not the issue. The fact remains that it has played this part, making us to some extent what we are today. What that role has been and how it has been played, and the more puzzling question of the role it could play in our present situation, are the questions to be explored.

Theology or religious thought, so conceived, is responsible to human society, not to the church. Its orientation is humanistic, not divine. Its norms must lie in the role which it performs in human life. In a certain sense, religious thought is to be evaluated pragmatically. The issue is not whether certain ideas or certain ways of expressing these ideas are faithful to some inherited standard or ancient text. It can scarcely be denied that the so-called Judaeo-Christian tradition has played an important part in shaping the culture of the West, but the question now has to do with the present function of that tradition. It was certainly part of our history. It had its place in our past. The real question is how it could have any place in the present and future, how it might be developed, interpreted or adapted to the present in such a way that religious thought might in some manner serve a constructive role in the further shaping of human life. Contemporary theology or religious thought must do justice, not to the form and content which it assumed in the context of the cultures into which it was born and took shape, but to those aspects of human life, variously conceived in different times and places, which have been and might still be the occasion of religious ideas. The central question, then, seems to be not what religion is, and certainly not what "religious truth" might be, but what religion has done for men and what it might do for men today.

Theology, so conceived, is a partner in a conversation

with the changing culture of man. If the conversation is to come alive, so that theology might make a critical and constructive contribution to it, then theology cannot be expected to remain unchanged in the process. The very possibility of a theological "orthodoxy," of an unchanging "faith of our fathers," is ruled out by the model of a lively conversation. Whatever insights into the "human situation" our religious past may provide us, therefore, can be helpful only insofar as we bring them into a dynamic conversation with and allow them to be influenced by the rapidly changing technological culture in which we live.

II

The Dissolution
of the Absolute

OURS IS AN INCREASINGLY SECULAR AGE, IT IS OFTEN SAID. Some see this development positively and draw our attention to what they take to be its values. Others see it negatively and stress the dangers, particularly the dangers to religion. The characterization of an age is a subject so vast and complex, and the judgments made about it can be of such varied sorts, that I should like to offer, as the only possible contribution which I can make to this subject, one man's analysis of what has been and is going on in the society and culture in which I live, as it bears upon the religious enterprise as I am familiar with it. I shall attempt to describe what has been and is happening, as I see it, to all of us in this society to a considerable extent and to some of us to a very great extent, whether we are concerned about the religious establishment or not. It may well be, when I have done, that I shall be said to have described only what has happened to me, and who can say whether his own case is typical or not? If others, instead of insisting that they do not see the world as I do—a point which seems hardly worth making—will tell us how they see their world, we may all end with a better understanding of where we are in relationshp to one another, and this may then be of some help to each of us in evaluating the "values" and "dangers" of our several ways of seeing the world in which we live. My purpose, then, is to describe how I see my own context, which will reveal, of course, how I see myself in that context. Perhaps it will be evident why I shall have said so little about the "values and dangers" of the context in which I live, or of my way of living in it and seeing it. Or perhaps it will be evident, to those with an eye for that sort of thing, that this was what I was doing all along, insofar as it makes any sense to speak of the "values and dangers" of being who one is.

The world in which I live, and apparently not alone, is a world which I should like to describe as following upon, or in the late stages of, a major socio-psychological shift in our culture, which I shall label "The Dissolution of the Absolute." It seems to have been the case, prior to this shift, that thoughtful men spoke not infrequently, and as though they had no thought of not being understood by their peers, of the Absolute, the Highest Good, or of Reality (with a capital R). This characteristic of language and thought has become increasingly difficult to maintain or recapture. The change has come about, so far as I can see, not as a result of a frontal assault on the idea of the Absolute, but by a process of dissolution or decay. The Absolute was not murdered, *Zarathustra* notwithstanding; it died of neglect.

The dissolution of the Absolute, the passing of a world view and a habit of thought, or its quiet displacement by another and different habit of thought, is a phenomenon that I have called a socio-psychological fact. With that label I wish to indicate how broad and basic a shift I have in mind, and how many ways there are of exploring and describing this change. One can, for example, ask about the causes and timing of the dissolution of that pattern of thought in which differing views about the

Absolute were held to be of such importance that these differences could lead to heresy trails and burnings at the stake, not to speak of wars. I take this question about the causes and timing of the change to be a historical question which it is the proper business of the historian of Western culture to explore. Setting dates for this sort of cultural shift is a rather arbitrary business, but let me just suggest, as an illustration of the historical aspect of the problem, that if one were to write a history of Western Christianity, it might be more accurate to locate the fundamental turning point not in the Reformation, as is so often the case with Protestant histories of Christianity, but somewhere nearer the French Revolution. After all, Luther and Calvin stand in one world with Augustine and Aquinas, no matter how they may disagree about the details; whereas none of them fit easily, if at all, into the world of the Enlightenment. The gap between the Reformers and the Scholastics is small indeed compared with the gap between them all and such men as Rousseau, Voltaire, or Jefferson.

One can also ask about the extent of the dissolution, to what extent it is the case that people no longer seem to operate on the assumption of an absolute. This is a question which the sociologists might be in as good a position as any to explore. Or, if they were willing to study our society with the penetration shown in their study of some other societies, perhaps cultural anthropologists could help us to see the extent to which our values, attitudes, and patterns of thought betray a departure from those in which words such as "God," "providence," "destiny," and "absolute" seemed to function powerfully. The social sciences could help us see to what extent the Absolute has been dissolved out of our operative images of life and the world.

Or one can ask about the shape of this changed situation, how it looks when the dissolution has taken place. This can be opened up to some extent by the social sciences, but it can also be exposed by the works of writers, poets, and artists. The question of shape is in part an aesthetic question, and insofar as a quantifiable answer seems to fall short of satisfying our questions, the artists, writers, literary and art critics, and aestheticians can help us to see where we are today.

Further, there is a task of clarifying the dissolution and the logic of our new situation, which is, from one point of view, a philosophical question. Metaphysics I take to be not some sort of super-science which might provide us with new information about the universe or "Reality" of a rather esoteric or subtle kind. I know that there are theologians who speak as if ontology were some sort of penetration of the "structure of being," but I gather that few if any philosophers are impressed by this. A metaphysics or ontology, as I gather it would be taken by most philosophers today, consists rather of a proposal, one might say an invitation, to see what we already know in a particular way. Metaphysics does not give us something new to see (such as "being itself" or "the ground of being") in any other way than by giving us a new way to see what we have been looking at all along.

32

From this point of view, then, to speak of the dissolution of the Absolute is one way of indicating a shift which has occurred in our metaphysical assumptions. At this point, however, I find that philosophers seem to withdraw from what I take to be a serious and worthwhile enterprise: the attempt to formulate and clarify the logic of the commonsense metaphysics of our society. They say, quite correctly, that a major piece of this job is not their business: namely, the careful empirical study of what people in our society think and the way in which they think. That would properly be the business of the behavioral and social sciences to discover. Yet when it comes to the task of formulating and analyzing the workings of our commonsense attitudes, it would seem to me that the philosopher need not be so retiring. The disdainful remark that the common sense of today is only the poor leavings of the best thinking of yesterday and beneath the dignity of philosophical investigation, which I have heard from several philosophers, bothers me a bit. After all, the common sense of today is the pattern of thinking in which we do our major arguing and debating of the great issues of our society. I notice that philosophers appear just about as frequently as theologians among the lists of those thinkers called upon by government and industry to assist in dealing with the major issues of our time. Could it be that philosophers as well as theologians, admittedly for different reasons, have simply opted out of the society of common sense? If theologians are the more irrelevant to life today, it is because they have been even more disdainful of the realm of ordinary language and ordinary common sense. Be that as it may, I would still wish to urge that there is a philosophical task to be performed in our attempts to get clear about the commonsense understandings of our time, and if this task is not well done by competent philosophers, then it will be poorly and sloppily done by others.

The dissolution of the Absolute, then, is a broad cultural shift which may be investigated and documented from a number of angles. It is a change that has affected our thought and language in ways so fundamental that they are not always noticed. Few have taken as little account of this shift as have the theologically inclined, although it should be evident that religion and theology are as much or more touched by the dissolution of the Absolute as any area of human activity. One consequence of failing to see this change that has taken place has been a certain degree of linguistic and logical confusion, resulting from attempting to operate in a world without absolutes while using ideas and languages drawn from a world in which the idea of the Absolute had an important place. The confusion is not unlike that of the substitute player in a football game rushing onto the field firmly clutching a baseball bat.

A prime example of this sort of confusion may be seen in the use of the word "reality." Now on any showing, this is a tricky word, an odd sort of noun, like "sadness" or "beauty," which is derived from a reasonably clear usage in the adjectival form of the word. That is to say, we do not seem to have much difficulty when we use the word "real." There is little difficulty knowing what we mean when we say that a mirage, the appearance of water on the road ahead on a hot summer day, is not real. Or in doing an elementary experiment in refraction, we may see that a stick half immersed in water looks bent; but we know, or so we say without confusion, that the stick is really straight, in spite of appearances. In these cases the words "real" and "really" serve the purpose of touching base in or reminding us of a commonly agreed frame of reference. Empirically minded though we may be, we are also aware of the limitations of sense experience. Our senses are not infallible, we say. Things are not always what they seem; skim milk masquerades as cream. But we do have words such as "seem," "appear," and "masquerade," and we do have the working distinction between the uses of these words and the use of the word "real," because we do have that common network of ground rules to which we are able to appeal with the word "real." If this, then, is how we use the word "real," what would be the meaning of "reality"? Well, in a great many cases "reality" is a word that refers to the whole of our understandings of how things are according to this same network of ground rules. So we might say that a man who is insane is a man who has "lost touch with reality." We mean that he no longer plays life's game according to the common rules. Or we say that a hypothesis seems "to conform to reality," by which we mean that it seems to fit fairly well into how we take things to be according to our commonly held understandings.

So far so good. That is, nothing is at all airtight about any of this, but we get along all right; we understand each other fairly well. Now along comes the knight of faith and speaks of "reality breaking in upon us"! Or he speaks to us in the name of "absolute reality," or, even more confusing, his faith is placed in "an objective reality." And here I would suggest that language has gone on a wild binge, which I think we should properly call a lost weekend.

This knight of faith is presumably speaking English, and so we take him to be using words which we have learned how to use. Only see what he does with them. "Reality," which is ordinarily used to call our attention once more to our agreements about how things are, is used now to refer to what the knight of faith must surely want to say is radically the opposite of all of our ordinary understandings. Why not better say, "Unreality is breaking in upon us"?

I think we can say something about what has gone wrong here. There was a time when the Absolute, God, was taken to be the cause of a great deal of what we would today call quite real phenomena, from rain and hail to death and disease. God was part of what people took to be the network of forces and factors of everyday existence, as real and as objective as the thunderbolts he produced. But today we no longer have the same reference for the word "reality." The network of understandings to which the word points has undergone important changes. The word "reality" has taken on an empirical

36

coloration which makes it now a bit confusing to speak of "reality breaking in upon us," unless we are referring to, for example, a sudden and unexpected visit from the police or a mother-in-law.

There is, however, another source of unclarity or confusion here, and that is the very fact of the dissolution of the Absolute itself. In the eleventh century the great theologian Anselm of Canterbury wrote a little essay containing an argument for the existence of God which continues to this day to occupy philosophers and theologians. I do not intend to explore Anselm's argument, but there is one contextual aspect of it which bears on our problem. Anselm was asking a certain question, the question about God, in such a way that he understood himself to be asking the one question which included and summed up every human question. And when he arrived at his answer, it was, as he conceived it, the discovery which was in some sense at once the answer to every human question. Indeed, I believe that this observation is true for all of the great traditional arguments for the existence of God. Those arguments were not trying to make a case for simply one entity, namely God, but for that which was the basis for and foundation of everything that is. Take away this frame of reference, this approach to these arguments, and they all become a bit silly.

Now the reason why most people today do regard these arguments as silly, the reason why we have difficulty accepting the answers or conclusions of these arguments, is because we simply do not know how to ask Anselm's question. We do not conceive it possible that there could be one answer which would entail and provide the answer to every question man can ask, in such diverse areas as, for example, politics, physics, mathematics, and aesthetics; so we are unable to ask after "God" in the way in which Anselm could. That being the case, we find it hard to accept his, or any of the arguments for the existence of God, as being persuasive. To speak of Absolute Reality is to speak in Anselm's world, not ours, both with respect to the word "Absolute" and to the word "Reality."

The change which I have called the dissolution of the Absolute has led to a pluralistic society and a pluralism of values and understandings. We are not in this world in one way; we live in our world in many ways, and it hardly seems to make sense to try to pull everything together under one heading. The sociologists call this differentiation, I believe, and another way of putting it would be to say that we have become relativists as well as pluralists. I am not saying, however, that we think everything is of the same or equal importance, or that we inhabit our various worlds or parts thereof in always the same and equal ways. Plurality does not entail equality of all the parts. It does mean, however, that life and the world are for us many different things, and that when we talk in a manner which convinces ourselves, we talk about "the whole" of life by talking in more detail or with more care about the various parts.

I touched on this in connection with Anselm's question and our inability to ask his question. The fact that

Anselm and his world are part of our past may be taken as a clue to what I would call our monistic hangover, which, when it is particularly acute, makes our pluralist waking an agony. The monistic images of our past haunt us in the most unexpected and sometimes unwanted places. We may find, for example, when we try to think or speak of the universe, that we do not honestly want to spell "universe" with a capital U. If we are asked about the extent of our small u universe, we may mention the rule of thumb which gives it a radius twice the range of the most powerful telescope, under the assumption that any presumed sources of light beyond that range are moving away from us at so nearly the speed of light that for all practical purposes (and isn't that a revealing phrase!) we can ignore them. And if we come closer to home, it is only out of habit that we speak of a "universe" at all. It really depends on how you approach it, we might say, for the "universe" of one discipline is but the background or a detail for another. All things considered, it appears to be more appropriate to speak of a polyverse.

But then that old monistic hangover begins to creep over us and tempts us to ask if there is not something fundamental to the human mind which leads us to keep on trying to pull things together, to see everything in some sort of interrelatedness, to devise laws and hypotheses in the hope of seeing how it all fits together into one whole. Perhaps at this point we need a bit of aspirin. Does the human mind actually do this, or is it more accurate to say that the human mind indeed tended to do this in the past out of which we have come? Perhaps we need to recall, for example, that historical study is one way of going at things, and it has developed and continues to develop its own methods. And physics is another way of going at things, with its own methods. And literary critics and biologists and painters also have their appropriate ways of exploring the world. Do we honestly think we shall come to understand any one of these ways, with its results, or indeed the whole of life, by somehow pulling them all together into one great system? When human knowledge was conceived of hierarchically—say on the model of a Gothic arch—it made sense to build comprehensive systems, and there could also be one queen of the sciences. But since the Gothic arch has been displaced by the marketplace as a model for human understanding, comprehensive systems have become strangely out of place, just as royalty finds itself out of a job in the context of the marketplace.

Pluralism means that we have granted that there are many ways of looking and seeing, many points of orientation, and that attempts to pull these all together into one grand scheme do not bring us closer to understanding how things are. The generalist has been displaced by the specialist in our society, in area after area of our common life. Insofar as this is true, insofar as this is how we think, we lose interest in Anselm's answer because we are not convinced he was asking the right question.

Relativism means that we appear to be coming more and more to a consensus that there is more than one way to look at any matter, and that what is said can be called true or false only in the terms provided by the particular point of reference. The student of art, for example, is encouraged to look at a given work of art in the light of the problems which the artist set for himself or were set for him by his situation. It is not a serious question for the student of art to ask what is the single greatest painting of all time.

Pluralism and relativism do not mean, however, that there are no distinctions to be made. One may have reasons for preferring one scale of values to another, one way of looking at a problem to another. But it is, I think we should agree, a mark of education and good sense to refrain from dogmatic statements which necessarily deny all merit to all other positions and points of view. One can hold serious commitments without universalizing them and without insisting that all who disagree are either knaves or fools. If relativism has an unpleasant sound, then let us call it tolerance. By whatever name, it is an important feature of the (secular) spirit of our age; and when we run into its denial, as in McCarthyism or Goldwaterism, most of us are at least uncomfortable. Somehow extremism has lost status, and if at moments it seems to make headway again, I think most of us regard this as a step backward, as a betrayal of what little progress civilization has made.

To ask theology and religion to accept the dissolution of the Absolute, to open their eyes to the world in which they live, is admittedly to ask much. It means that religion must not only become much more guarded in speaking of God (if not give this up altogether); it means also that more care be exercised in speaking of "unique revelation," "absolute commitment," and some single "ultimate concern." It is to ask of the life of faith that it be lived as a certain posture, involving commitments, but held in balance with many other commitments; a certain willingness to see things in a certain way without feeling obliged to say that this is the only way in which they can be seen. The question may fairly be asked whether theology and faith can survive this shift of focus; whether Christianity, for example, which has for so long proclaimed a monistic view of the universe, a single and unique point of reference as the only valid one, with a single and unique revelation of this truth, can learn to live in a world from which the Absolute has been dissolved. However one may choose to answer this in theory, we are in fact in the actual process of finding this out, for living when we do and as we are is not exactly a matter of choice. What are the values and dangers of this? Well, what are the values and dangers of being alive? They are the values and dangers of being who we are.

III

What Do We Mean
by "An Empirical Investigation
of the Church"?

THE PURPOSE OF THIS PAPER IS TO THROW LIGHT ON THE
question of what Christians are talking about when
they talk about the Church. The question to which it is
addressed asks about the procedures which would be appropriate for an empirically minded Christian to use in
investigating the Church. As the question is phrased, it
raises a number of subsidiary questions. Who is this
"we"? How well does the term "empirical" describe the
sort of investigation which would be appropriate to this
"we"? To what does the word "church" refer? And finally,
what is the relationship of speaking of the Church "empirically" to speaking of it "theologically"?

The argument, if such it can be called, will, by the
nature of the case, take the form of a bid for your agreement that the term "empirical" points to our human experience as a common ground on which we might all, or
most of us, be willing to meet, and on which we tend to
rely, and that it is on this common ground of experience
that we might productively carry out our discussions
about the Church. If the case for this "playing field" is
persuasive, you may be willing to follow the suggestion
that this first move implies a method for clarifying how
we talk about the Church, which will be illustrated with
reference to the exerience of a friendship and of a conversation, and finally, with reference to our experience of
other Christians. The suggestion will be that all of our
language about the Church, theological language included, can be understood as playing on this same field,
and that this understanding of how we talk about the

45

Church may overcome the schizophrenic character of much contemporary ecclesiology.

The word "empiricism" may call to your minds different things. For some it calls forth the shades of Locke and Hume, for others it suggests methodology, for others a way of pointing to a widespread feature of contemporary thought. I should like to try to pull these different threads together and suggest for the purposes of this paper a way to use this word. First of all, it should be noted that contemporary empiricism, as a philosophical position, is far less rigid and mechanical in its conception of the empirical footing of statements of truth than the early British empiricists. It has moved away from the insistence of a Locke or a Hume that every word that has meaning must have a sensible reference. Contemporary empiricists, such as Quine, perhaps under the not surprising influence of developments in the natural sciences, recognize a broader and a softer commitment to sensible experience than that. The empiricist today is not liable to say "Show me" at the sound of every word, nor even at the end of every sentence or every paragraph. He does, however, expect that the whole network of his understanding, be it of atomic structure, light, society or human activity, should "touch base" in sense experience at important points. At least along the edges, so to speak, a network of hypotheses should be anchored in experience, available to the scrutiny of any who are concerned and equipped to check the validity of the network in question. An empiricist is not one to ask either the social investigator or the theologian to "nail down" each and every statement with empirical data. He will ask, however, that there be enough contact with experience to give a grounding for the whole subject of discussion, and if that can be established, he will be satisfied. If it is granted that some kinds of empirical evidence will seriously affect the whole pattern of the picture, and if no part of the picture is immune to the results of empirical investigation made along the edges, then such a picture may be judged to be empirically meaningful.

Thus far I have talked about empiricism as a procedure or method. I have done so in such a way as to indicate that I feel "at home" with this sort of method, that I find I take seriously the results of such a method, and that if it were ignored I should not be comfortable with the results. An investigation of a city, a small group, or an individual by empirical methods is one that would "make sense" to me. It would "make sense" to me because it assumes, and rightly so, that the investigator and I both respect experience. Behind the technical-sounding word "empiricism" stands the more general term of experience to which it appeals, and I accept the sort of "soft empiricism" described because I assume, for all practical purposes (and isn't *that* a revealing phrase!), that things are the way I experience them. This metaphysical assumption about the way things are, I want to suggest, is widely shared in Western society today. To challenge this assumption is to challenge the way in which I tend to think in all areas of life, and I can frankly only urge the admission from us all that we share in this assumption to a high degree. If you do not agree with this, then I must grant at once that the rest of this paper will be of no help to you.

Let me make one more point in this connection. If we agree that we do in practice grant a privileged status to experientially supported networks of understanding, if we are "soft empiricists" in the way in which I have suggested, an important part of our experience is the difference, reflected in the structure of our language, between "I" and "he" or "they." The linguistic peculiarities of the first person singular pronoun have been explored by empirically minded philosophers and they have helped me to see that my death for me, for example, is quite another matter than my death for you.[1] Indeed, to experience something is always in one sense personal, and while we find it important to check our experiences against those of others, nevertheless I should want to say that my own experience of something is never reducible for me to things which I share with others who experience that same phenomenon. And finally, my own experience of myself is not reducible for me to what others experience of me. I suggest that Christians have a vested interest in insisting on this distinction between first person and third person experience. I mention it here as an element in my metaphysical assumption about how things are, which is part of my soft empiricism and which I wish to suggest is an assumption on which we might all be willing to agree.

The outlines and markings of the proposed playing field might best be clarified by trying a few games on it. Let us begin with the game of friendship. John knows Bill well and the relationship has ripened to the point at which John calls Bill his friend. His experience of Bill is as a friend, we might say. Tom, a third person, does not know Bill in this way. For him Bill is simply another man. Now of course John will admit that Bill is indeed another man, but because of past experiences, he wants to say, "But Bill is more than that. He is a friend." When Tom finds he cannot say this, he indicates that there is no relationship between Bill and himself.

Suppose now that John tries to explain to Tom why he speaks as he does of Bill. He might recount numerous situations in which he and Bill were involved, he might try to give an exhaustive account of all Bill's features which attract him. The most that he could expect from Tom would be the admission that these reports did help Tom to see why John called Bill a friend. They could not lead Tom himself to call Bill a friend. Only his own experience with Tom could lead to that.

So much for our first game. Now let's try one a bit more complex, called "having a conversation." How do you have a conversation? I suppose I had better say, a *real* conversation, one of those conversations that has no conclusion, where there is real meeting of minds and spirits, where you come away, reluctantly, and remember that moment for a long time afterwards. If I put side by side, as it were, two good conversations which I have had in the past year, what do they have in common? Well, I can point to some common features. As I said, neither had an end nor conclusion. Neither has been forgotten. Both took place in a relatively quiet place, free from interruptions. Both were with friends. The longer I make the list of features of a conversation, however, the more dissatisfied I become. None of these features seem to get at the heart of the matter. I can control these various features, to some extent. I can set up the same sort of context again but I cannot make the talk turn into a conversation the next time, and it is just this factor or element which I can't define, to which I can only point in a rather unsatisfactory manner by using words such as "spirit," or "moment," which makes all the difference. In fact, having said all this, I reveal that I cannot say *how* you have a conversation. So if I want to tell someone else what a conversation is, after all my talking around the subject, I have to say, "Well, it's not just all that. In order to know what a conversation is you have to have one."

With these little practice sessions as a warm-up, let us now turn to the subject of talking about the Church. In fact, as will become evident, I should want to say we have already eased into this game by the fact of playing on this field which I have been trying to make a bit clearer by playing these games. Let's pick up the ball where we left it with John, Bill and Tom. Let John now be a Christian, and Bill will be a group of people which we will call the Church. The term "friend" will become terms such as "Body of Christ," "People of God," and the like. Tom is a nonbeliever. The sort of investigation of the Church which would interest the Christian would be one which centered on those features of that group, or perhaps of individuals within it, which have attracted the Christian, together with past experiences he has had with this group, or with people whom he associates with the group, which lead him to be to some degree committed to it. Such an investigation will include everything that the nonbeliever can discover, if he wishes to look, and it will include nothing that the nonbeliever cannot investigate, if he so desires. But the believer will insist on a certain constellation of aspects to be investigated which is defined by his own experiences with other believers, separately and together. Nevertheless, I want to point out that nobody is leaving the playing field at any point.

The question must be asked, however, in the light of our game about conversations, will there be any way in which we might discover, by means of examining a believer's relationships and experiences in the past with this group, what it is that might lead him to call the Church "the Body of Christ"? He could tell an interested observer of past experiences he has had with one or more fellow Christians which has led him to speak as he does of the whole group of Christians. We might detect in many cases that his references for such experiences touch the local congregation or the parish, or the whole of his communion, only indirectly. It may be that because he has experienced a certain unity with one or more believers, a unity which overcomes other grounds for disunity, he has as it were extended the experience and referred it to the larger group because, perhaps, he and the others involved in this experience were all members of this group. Before we can say more about this, we would have to do some investigating.

The question about the reference for so-called theological assertions about the Church raises the question of how that word "church" is to be used. It is, I believe, evident that the word "church" has a fairly well-established use in the English language. Insofar as we are speaking English, and not some game of speaking translated-first-century Greek, when we say "church" we ordinarily refer to a religious institution, with its buildings and its professional staff, perhaps at times including the dues-paying members who support the institution and are on its lists. We go to church, we join a church, we wish the church would speak up or shut up or do something. All these common remarks refer to a religious institution. I do not believe it is about this institution, in any simple direct way, that Christians make their theological assertions. Usually, it would seem, they make the assertions of ecclesiology about the Christians, people marked by Christian faith, presumably, people who go, among other places, to church. If we sort out our language in this way, then one can see that it is one thing to talk about Christians having a mission, being involved in daily life, and all that sort of thing, but it is quite another thing, to my mind a most unfortunate thing, to say that the religious institution should be involved in the world or have a mission. If we use the word "church" in both senses, with these two different references, as a word both in the English language *and* in translated-first-century Greek, we shall probably only confuse ourselves and others. Indeed, I believe that we have already.

My suggestion for bringing at least a little order into the game of talking about the Church is that we accept the common usage of the word "church," letting it refer to a building, a religious institution, and its professional staff, and speak of the Christians as simply the Christians. If this distinction is allowed for the purposes of this stage of the argument, it may then be suggested that the assertions of ecclesiology arise among Christians with reference to their experiences with one or more other Christians. When this language is applied *directly* to the religious institution, we should not be surprised if the result is at least paradoxical.

This distinction leaves open the question of the relation of the Christians to the church (still speaking English), and on this point I am sure I have many more questions than answers. If one Christian has had an experience of reconciliation with another Christian, what might lead him to speak of the gathering of Christians as a fellowship of reconciliation? Is it because Christians are almost always members of churches? Is it because he thinks that something that goes on in churches contributes in some way to these other experiences of reconciliation? It seems to me that we are not far removed from the question of the relationship between planning a party, and having it really come off as a bang-up evening, of arranging a conversation, and actually having a real conversation. It is not simply that these experiences of reconciliation are more than goes on in church, or that language of ecclesiology refers, perhaps, primarily to these experiences rather than to the religious institution. Even if we could decide that the assertions of theology about the church actually seemed to refer to these experiences, we would have the same difficulty we had in trying to define a real conversation. And I would insist that it is truly the same difficulty, one of the hazards of this playing field, in no sense to be solved by quitting this field for another. (I am afraid that the grass only *looks* greener on some other field.)

We began by asking about an empirical investigation of the church. Let me outline what I think that might be, in the light of these considerations, and see what role the assertions of ecclesiology would play. The outline will remain on the field on which I have suggested we all stand, in a meadow called experience, on which the lines of our empirical playing field are laid out. Let us begin with theological assertions which Christians make about the church, so that we can agree as fellow Christians about what we want to investigate, for that is the largest part of the problem. Let me take just two of the four creedal affirmations about the church, that the church is one and that it is apostolic. I recognize that there is no universal agreement in any terms about the meaning of these claims. For the sake of illustrating the method, however, let me pick one interpretation of each word.

When a man says that the church is one, I suggest that behind this assertion lies one or more experiences with one or more fellow believers, perhaps from rather different denominational, class or national backgrounds, where there has been a sense of unity or reconciliation across this barrier. Having discovered this unity with other Christians, he affirms that they are one. What matters most to him is the fact that they have found themselves to be one, and the other things which divide them are pushed into second place. An empirical investigation of the church, as Christians might be interested in conducting it, would begin from this so-called theological assertion and explore the situations which arise from time to time in which Christians discover this unity, and then go on to explore the extent to which these experiences bear upon other things which Christians do separately and together, and vice versa. Do these experiences have any effects on his involvements in the religious institution? What is there about the religious institution that might account for or bear on such experiences of unity? An empirical investigation of the church should be able to throw some light on these questions.

Again, when a man asserts that the church is apostolic, I suggest that behind this assertion lies one or more experiences of recognizing the testimony of the apostles as in some way normative in conversations which he has had with other believers about the character or implications of that peculiar perspective upon life which is called faith. They found, let us say, that in sharing this perspective and exploring its implications, the picture of Jesus

Christ painted by the New Testament authors weighed importantly in the conversation, or they at least tried to let the apostolic testimony have a decisive voice in the conversation. On such an interpretation of apostolicity, and I am aware that there are other interpretations, an empirical investigation of the church will begin with this creedal assertion and explore the situations which arise from time to time in which Christians discover an important place for the apostolic writings in their conversations, and will go on to discover the effects which this has on other things which they do together and separately, and on their relationships to the religious institution, and vice versa.

On this interpretation, an empirical investigation of the church would be an investigation appropriate to the playing field on which I suggest almost all of us today play almost all of life's games, but it would at the same time be an investigation of precisely those features and those moments of the lives of Christians which appear to lead them to make the odd theological affirmations which they make about the church. It would be an exploration of the dynamics of those conversations between two or more members of the church, in which (to include all four of the creedal affirmations) elements of unity or reconciliation, purpose or task, historical continuity or insight, and apostolic or biblical importance affect the conversation and other actions in which Christians are involved separately and together, including their involvement in the religious institution. These conversations and experiences are as open to any other investigator as they are to a Christian, and they are as closed to the Christian as they are to any investigator who seeks to know what it is that makes a real conversation, and in just the same way. In this way we remain on the playing field of empirical method, laid out on the broad meadow of experience, the game to be played being an exploration of the assertions of Christian faith concerning the church and their experiential references.

Current literature on the church reflects a growing interest in empirical studies of the church and of religious attitudes in general which is appropriate to our contemporary assumptions about experience. An analysis of "the church as a human community" does not stirke us as out of place today. I suggest that the results of such studies, that is, the empirical results, would be widely accepted today. The problem arises from the fact that many such studies are by men who make use of theological affirmations about the church and make the logical mistake of thinking that the religious institution, the majority of whose members, let us say, do not wish to admit Negroes, is the proper point of reference for such an assertion as, "the Church is Mission," in caps. Having made this identification, it is not surprising that they are shocked by the discrepancy between empirical finding and theological affirmation.

H. Richard Niebuhr's proposal for the solution of this muddle may be taken as typical of contemporary ecclesiology in this country, at least for those who take theological affirmations seriously because they are Christians, and who take empirical findings seriously by virtue of the playing field on which we all seem to play today. I would suggest that the proposal is misleading. Niebuhr's suggestion was the use of what he called "the method of polar analysis; that is, (that we) must try to do justice to the dynamic character of that social reality, the Church, by defining certain poles between which it moves or which it represents."[2]

To take what seem to be rather selective and limited empirical findings about the religious institution and its constituency on the one hand, and theological affirmations on the other, as two poles, suggests the model of a magnetic field, or possibly the two foci of an elipse. But Niebuhr and others in fact approach what they call the two poles with quite different methods. The alternative which I am suggesting is that we begin with the theological assertions and assume that we are already playing on the field of experience. The task, then, is to investigate empirically the sorts of situations which might account for these affirmations, and not simply those characteristics of the religious institution and its constituency which might be made about any institution in our society. All the latter findings may well be true. If we really want to know what the church is and how it functions, however, it is too superficial to discover that it caters to an exclusive ingroup, for example, which makes no important contribution to the solving, say, of the problem of the modern metropolis. We should hardly expect it to, and certainly, I would argue, the affirmations of ecclesiology do not suggest that this institution *should* make any *direct* contribution in this area. The question worth exploring, however, is the bearing of the experiences, conversations, and the like, of Christians, which lead them to speak as they do of their unity, mission, etc., to the religious institution, and, more importantly, to other areas of their life in the metropolis.

NOTES

[1] William H. Poteat, "I Will Die: An Analysis," *The Philosophical Quarterly*, January 1959.
[2] H. Richard Niebuhr, *The Purpose of the Church and its Ministry*, New York, Harper and Row, 1956, p. 19.

IV

Christian Education
in a
Pragmatic Age

THE FOLLOWING ARTICLE IS WRITTEN IN RESPONSE TO A request to develop the implications for Christian education of the approach to and interpretation of Christian faith represented in my book, *The Secular Meaning of the Gospel*. I intend neither to summarize nor defend the argument of that book, but, in the light of further reflection since it was written, I do wish to touch briefly on two aspects of that interpretation, by way of clarifying the point of view of this article. Then, after making clear how I intend to use the term "Christian education," I shall develop programmatically the implications of the one for the other.

The argument of my book suffers from two major limitations, or at least there are two problems which beg for fuller and more careful development. One has to do with metaphysical assumptions, and the other has to do with our interest in the past. A word addressed to each of these problems may serve to indicate the approach to be used here.

The argument of my book rests on the acceptance of what could be called the metaphysics of "So what?": a way of seeing the world and of understanding how things are, which seems to be operative for most of us in the West most of the time. When we ask "so what?" in response to something said to us, we are asking for the implications or consequences of that which has been said, or of that which is said to be the case. The kinds of responses which we take to be answers to our question, as opposed to those which strike us as evasions or nonsense, reveal our operative understandings of the way things are, of what is "real" and what matters to us. This configuration or network of understandings I take to be the "going" metaphysical assumption of our culture.

If asked for more precision about the character of this metaphysics, I am willing to answer that it is somewhat empirical, somewhat pragmatic, somewhat relativistic, somewhat naturalistic, but also somewhat aesthetic and somewhat personalistic. My answer is intentionally vague, in order to make clear that the metaphysics in the terms of which I have developed my interpretation of faith is meant to be descriptive. I wish neither to defend nor attack this way of seeing the world and ourselves in it. I do suggest that it is possible to clarify a descriptive metaphysics which is characteristic of our age, and if I have misrepresented it, I should be glad to be corrected. In any case, it is in the terms provided by this framework that I have tried to develop my interpretation of the language of faith. Probably the only case that can be made for relying on this commonsense metaphysics lies in appealing to its descriptive character, for that is the basis of saying that it is more widely shared than are the metaphysical assumptions of, e.g., Biblical Theology, Thomism or Heidegger. Whether the pattern and presuppositions of our daily thinking ought to be what they seem to be is not a question I have argued. I have assumed that we do see the world in certain ways, that our culture has what can be called a loose metaphysics, and for the purposes of doing theology today, I have proposed that we explore the possibilities of standing on this common ground. If faith has an argument with culture, if it evaluates elements of human life and culture negatively, still it will, on my interpretation, conduct this argument in the terms provided by this common ground.

These remarks indicate that I am looking at metaphysics not as some sort of super-science which might provide us with new information about the "universe" or "reality" (cf. J. Heywood Thomas contra Tillich). Rather, I am assuming that any and every metaphysics is a proposal, an invitation, to see what we already know in a particular way. Metaphysics does not give us something new to see in any other way than by giving us a new way to see what we have been looking at all along (cf. John Wisdom).

The metaphysical status of Christian faith is odd. Faith would appear to entail a certain way of seeing the world and this would seem to make a contribution to a believer's network of understandings. The terms of that network, however, are shared (in my view of faith) with unbelieving contemporaries. My interpretation of Christian faith, therefore, is an attempt to portray the contribution it makes to a believer's network of understandings, insofar as it does not provide new "facts," new information, or assume the presence of entities (such as gods or God) lying beyond the general framework of the descriptive metaphysics of our time and place. An attempt to make sense out of the language of faith and theology in the terms of a contemporary descriptive metaphysics can

65

have no other status than that of an invitation to see the matter in one way, and the double use of the definite article in the title of my book should not be taken as implying that I was attempting or doing more (or less) than that.

The second problem lies in the dependence of my interpretation on the past, on the history of Jesus and of Easter. It may be argued, however, that one feature of contemporary secular culture is its almost exclusive concern with contemporaneity: the past is not of great moment to most of us most of the time. Moreover, does not Christian faith qualify an interest in the past, leading us to say, in various ways, that the past is of no avail unless it becomes "somehow" contemporaneous with the believer? It would have been more honest to the tradition and also to contemporary thought if I had argued that in fact it is not the historical event which becomes an occasion for "discernment" for the believer, but rather the *story* of the event, or even the image of Jesus which is portrayed by the contemporary church in its preaching and worship.

This present image of the church is one which is constantly changing with the changing cultural context of the church. When Christians today speak of Jesus as a man involved in history and "the world," they speak out of a context which sees history and society in certain ways which influence the way they see man. Marx and Freud have played their part in defining the image of Jesus as "the man-for-others," and the development in the nineteenth century of the Western understanding of man separates a Bonhoeffer, a Barth and a Bishop Robinson from a Luther, a Calvin and a Bishop Jewel. Certainly the contemporary picture of Jesus is also produced by the fact that the contemporary church reads with contemporary eyes the writings of the New Testament, but perhaps a relative and pluralistic appreciation of something like the Catholic conception of historical tradition would help broaden a too naïve dependence upon the past. With these qualifications or clarifications of the empirical and—let us say it—a-theistic interpretation of the language of faith which I have made, let us turn to the subject of "Christian education."

Education, Christian or otherwise, is a word which may be used in a number of ways. It can be used so broadly, and it frequently is, that it includes within it almost all of life. We do speak of "the school of life," "education of the whole man," and "education for life." If Christian education means education as sponsored by the Christian churches in this broad sense, everything which the churches and Christians do could be considered as Christian education, including at least preaching, worship, praying, evangelism, missions, discipline, and family life, as well as Sunday School and adult classes. I wish to make it clear that I have no intention of speaking to a subject as broad as that. Instead, *for the purposes of this article, I shall take education to refer to planned pro-*

grams of instruction, to what we ordinarily think of when we speak of teachers and students, books and classrooms. In short, I want to allow for a variety of activities in life, one of which, and only one of which, is education. By taking this narrower use, I acknowledge the pluralism of modern life, within which the activities of the churches are only a part, and within which part Christian education is taken to be only a part. I exclude from my consideration, for example, the teaching done by a Christian employed to teach in a college or university, not because I deny that his work may also be called "Christian education," but because I want to focus the problem narrowly. Unless clarity can be gained in the narrow case, I fear confusion will be compounded in the broader cases. My focus, therefore, shall be on Sunday Schools, so-called, adult classes, and similar formal means of instruction which make up part of the planned activities of normal congregations.

The question to which I shall address myself, then, is this: insofar as "believers" share the commonsense metaphysical commitments of our age, and insofar as their faith functions in the way I have indicated, i.e., within the terms of those metaphysical assumptions (and I am aware, of course, that there are those who would not accept the adequacy of either of these conditions), what are the possibilities and limitations of the teaching work, as distinct from the preaching and worship, of the churches, of religious organizations and their professional or voluntary staff?

Christian education is planned instruction in the service of Christian faith. In that service, the teacher can (1) teach the Christian story, and as a story, (2) clarify the relations between faith and knowledge, and (3) clarify the relations between believing and living. In summary, he can teach "about" Christian faith in a way comparable to teaching "about" love.

Near the end of an essay entitled "The Choice of Comrades," Ignazio Silone compares the spiritual condition of himself and others with a refugee encampment in no-man's land. "What do you think refugees do from morning to night? They spend most of their time telling one another the story of their lives."[1] Christians have continued and have led others to join them through telling and retelling an "old, old story," which they tell as being in some peculiar way the story also of their own lives. They tell this story and their faith lives off this story. He who performs the work of Christian education serves faith by teaching this story, making it familiar, tracing different ways in which it can be and has been told. He does not *tell* the story itself. That is for pulpit and holy table. He teaches the story as a story.

He teaches the story. It is nothing short of amazing that preachers still use, in whatever way, biblical texts, still make references to biblical passages. What sense can this make to those who do not even know the stories of the Bible? In order that the particular story or the particular form of the whole Christian story which is being told at any one time may be heard with even a fraction of the fullness which the preacher intends, it is necessary that the listeners know the whole range of biblical stories. If they do not learn these stories in Sunday School or Bible class, where shall they learn them? What is Easter without the story of Mary and the Gardener and also the story of the Exodus? What is Christmas without the Nativity stories of both Matthew and Luke? What is Christian love without the stories of the Good Samaritan and of Lazarus and the rich man? Stories can be taught and learned. That is the task of Christian education.

Christian education involves the teaching of the stories of Christian faith as stories. If refugees spend most of their time telling the story of their lives, it is because telling stories does something which listing statistics does not. A good story, which as a story serves a certain purpose, may no longer serve that purpose if transposed into a "record of facts," whatever that may be. If believers are to benefit by hearing the Christian story, it might be well for them to be shown that stories have important functions to perform. Deprive man of his stories, make him unable to tell and hear stories, and you make him by that much a poorer creature.

Men do other things besides telling stories. They also collect facts, as we say, and they also do critical historical investigation, at many different levels. You can collect "facts," as it were, related in various ways, it may be argued, to the founding of the Plymouth colony. You may attempt to get at the critical historical account of the Pilgrims' lives and times. In addition you can tell the story of the Pilgrim Fathers, having to do with, e.g., the celebration of Thanksgiving Day. The story is not the same as facts and not the same as critical history, but it can do something which neither of the others can. It can give an American a way to tell about the origin of his country and about himself all at once. Stories are appropriate to celebration, and celebration is important to being human. Indeed, stories are one of man's great ways of understanding himself. As Silone continued: "The stories are anything but amusing, but [refugees] tell them to one another, really, in an effort to make themselves understood."

He who serves in the work of Christian education serves faith, therefore, by teaching the role which storytelling plays in human life, in the hopes of winning a frame of mind that will appreciate stories, not as "facts," not as "critical history," but as stories, as one of men's important ways of winning understanding and of being understood.

Christian faith finds expression in language. It is expressed in other ways as well, but with respect to faith, as with respect to so many of man's concerns and activities, language is one of the principle ways in which we communicate with one another. Believers, when speaking as believers, have said all sorts of peculiar things. They have said "Jesus is Lord," "glory to God in the Highest," and "I believe in the Holy Spirit and eternal life." But believers have spoken as ordinary men, in ways which do not seem particularly to express Christian faith, in saying such things as "Johnson is President," "Three cheers for the Yankees," and "I believe in the graduated income tax and old-age pensions." There seem to be no important relations between these two sets of sentences. Is it because the second set is about concrete things and persons which all of us or many of us care about, whereas the former set has to do with another world? Or put the question another way. I know that Johnson is President. Do I know that Jesus is Lord? In each case, how? In each case, what sort of knowing am I talking about? These questions indicate the task of Christian education in serving faith by clarifying the relation between faith and knowledge.

It is a commonplace to say that most churchgoers are either wrong or confused about the nature of faith. Some take faith as assent to a group of peculiar assertions, as did the Red Queen when she said she had mastered the art of believing six impossible things before breakfast. Others take faith to be a sort of inner glow that makes you feel good all over. Since the language of faith, traditionally, is so often associated with things which no man has ever seen, it is not surprising if a somewhat empirical age finds faith to be at best a bit fuzzy. All of this is widely known and often decried. Little seems to be done about it. Whatever can be done about it, it is the task of those engaged in Christian education to help untangle the mess so that churchgoers might at least have some idea of the logical placing of the language of faith and so have some idea of what faith is and isn't.

One way in which this untangling might begin is by calling peoples' attention to other areas of human experience which lead to similar linguistic problems of unclarity, misunderstanding and imprecision. If churchgoers find religious language puzzling, they ought to take a look at the language of art criticism, to give just one example. If they think that faith is sometimes at its best without verbalization, they should ponder the masses of people who today flood art museums. If one compares aesthetic experience, if there is such, and religious experience, if there is such, if one reflects on the suggestion that museums have replaced or are becoming the contemporary form of cathedrals, one might at least be opened to entertaining a fresh consideration of the workings of religious language.

The privileged status which we seem to have conferred on the natural sciences, however accurately or inaccurately understood, has for many led to an odd association of knowledge with fact, which is, when you come to think of it, exceedingly odd. Be that as it may, it takes a bit of stirring up for most of us today to be reminded that in science itself, in poetry, in doing history, and in philosophy, there are many occasions when language seems to come up against its limits, as it were. That is to say, there are many areas of human experience—think of falling in love—when we have all sorts of difficulties saying what would be appropriate and would do justice to the occasion. Try telling a friend about the painting which came alive for you that afternoon you "really saw it for the first time" (something you might well say of a painting which you had looked at a dozen times). Try to explain how it is you can recognize a good friend in a crowd. Try to tell your beloved how much you love him or her.

Learning about art and about talking about art is something which is not in principle impossible for contemporary man. Courses in art appreciation can develop a certain sensitivity, can teach one to look with greater care, can lead one by comparison to become aware of the variety of ways in which artists have set problems for themselves and gone about solving those problems. Learning about religion need not be any more difficult, though it may not be any easier, and it may be facilitated by awakening an appreciation for comparable features in other learning games, such as learning about art, about duty, about music, about love. Are these areas in which it seems appropriate to use words such as "know," "fact," "prove"? In some parts, yes, and in most parts, no. If an appreciation for the problems of clarity in these areas were aroused, a great step forward would have been made in leading the horse to water. You can't, we are told, make the horse drink, but it would be helpful if the horse and the water were, so to speak, at least formally introduced to each other, so that the horse may realize that water is not something you rake into a pile before beginning to consume it.

Those engaged in Christian education can serve Christian faith by clarifying the relation between believing and living. Christians have long insisted that how a man believes affects how he lives. One of them once said that if any man says that he loves God and at the same time hates his brother, he is a liar, and another early believer called Christianity "the way." On the other hand, believers frequently disagree about the precise consequences of believing when it comes to specific decisions. This disagreement appears to have led many Christians to conclude that the relationship between believing and living is so vague or general that nothing specific can be said, or even that faith has no concrete ethical consequences at all. We face today some of the painful consequences of this conclusion in the present sorry state of churches in which many believers see no conflict between Christian faith and the practice of racial discrimination.

As a contribution to clearing away confusions in these and similar areas, it could be the task of those involved in Christian education to help identify the ethical assumptions and practices of the society in which we live, assumptions about law, politics and government, about economics, automation and technology, about social, economic and racial groups, and about sex and its relation to the rest of life. If, by the use of the case method and other means designed to keep the problems specific, contemporary attitudes and assumptions of our society could be brought out into the open and identified, one would at least be in a position in which it would be interesting— and possibly exciting—to develop the implications of believing that the Sabbath was made for man, that the neighbor is the occasion for love, and that human personhood is of unsurpassable importance. Clarification of the assumptions of our society and the development of specific implications of Christian faith, with the initiation of reflection on whether and how they are related, is a task which could well be performed under the heading of Christian education.

In conclusion: Christian education involves teaching "about" Christian faith in a way which is comparable to teaching "about" love. I should think that most people would agree that you cannot "teach love," that this combination of words does not go well together. You can love another person, and he may then respond with love, but it would also be rather awkward and inappropriate to say he had then learned "how to love." Love can, however, be "taught about."

How would you go about teaching about love? You might begin with the literature of love—love stories of ancient and more modern vintage. You might go on to the histories or stories of great lovers, including the reading of their letters. Then you could turn to the poetry of love. Finally, you could add other ways of talking about love —the analyses of anthropologists and psychiatrists— ways which would hardly be those of lovers. The differences between these various kinds of language are worth exploring.

In making this analogy, I do not wish to say that faith is in all respects of the same order as love. Like love, it is a human posture, a commitment, a way of seeing some people and things (but probably not a vision which governs all of man's thinking and activity in every realm of his existence), and it entails certain actions. Unlike love, however, its object is not at hand. Believers have stories to tell, not a photograph to look at. Since the modern era and the rise of the critical historical imagination, Christians have had to find analogies for the object of faith in myth, story and parable. They have always had to do this, but until fairly recent times they could always pretend that their faith somehow gave them an insight into "ultimate truth." Now that classical Western theism has been shaken, and with it the justification of faith, unjustifiable faith must live by faith alone, and in this sense it is not unlike love. Human love, therefore, provides a helpful analogy to human faith, and in this sense, those engaged in Christian education have the task of teaching "about" faith.

NOTES

1 *Encounter*, Vol. III, No. 6, Dec., 1954, p. 28.

V

On Doing Theology

AT THE CONCLUSION OF THIS PAPER, THE APPROPRIATE response may well consist of a nervous cough and an embarrassed silence, broken finally by someone turning to his neighbor and saying, "Now about that point you were making a little while back. . . ." Which is to say, I am not at all sure that my paper is even on the same subject as the rest of this discussion, much less a contribution to it. Having rashly accepted to address myself to the theme "the problem of nonobjectifying thinking and speaking in contemporary theology," I find that I really do not want to speak about this at all, which may account in part for the way I intend to proceed. I intend to poke around in the outer edges of our topic, just to make it clear that I really do not know how to come at it, and then turn and wander off in another direction and talk a bit about talking, and then, to show I am not simply a coward, to rush back and have another go at the topic before retiring and giving my own version of the glorious battle which I have won. I concede at once that my opponent may not even have noticed my attack, let alone think that someone was trying to do battle with him. No doubt he will tell his version of the battle (if such indeed it can be called) in his own way.

Mr. Ott, if I understand him correctly, has a certain understanding of language which he has taken from Heidegger and which plays no small part in his conception of how to do theology. Having been told that Mr. Ott's essay, "What is Systematic Theology?", was to be taken as the background for this colloquium, I have tried to see what his problem of "objectifying" and "non-objectifying" language is, and I must confess that the matter is not altogether clear to me. I gather that the matter is not altogether clear for him either, for he concludes, in his response to his American critics, that he himself does not know what "objectifying thinking and speaking" is. (212) Mr. Ott's uncertainty about his own problem makes it all the more difficult for me to see the issue with any clarity.

When I run into these sorts of confusions, I turn almost automatically to the advocates and practitioners of a certain way of doing philosophy, who at times, and to the disgust of their critics, have claimed to have no other concern than winning a bit of clarity about our use of language. Perhaps clarity is not enough, but surely in a matter such as this a bit of clarity would do no harm, even if it did no more than suggest other ways of stating the problem with which we think we are bothered. Mr. Ott's problem has to do with language, as he understands language. It may be helpful—or it may be at least diverting—to look to these other thinkers about language, for they have frustrated many and bored others by talking about nothing but language, or so at least it has often seemed. Be that as it may, a little linguistic analysis seems to me to be much needed in this discussion.

What bothers me, however, is that the really competent analysts of language seem to have made no serious effort to enter into conversation with Heidegger. If a conversation has not gotten off the ground between the later

Wittgenstein (to be Continental) and the later Heidegger, nor between any of their fellow practitioners of their
several ways of doing philosophy, it seems foolhardy for
an amateur in their game to try what the professionals
have deemed best not to attempt. But (with apologies to
Augustine of Canterbury), let fools rush in where Angles
fear to tread!

Mr. Ott's understanding of language is taken, he tells
us, from the later Heidegger. Rather than attempt an
immanent critique of this understanding, let me instead
offer an alternative way of thinking about language, and
we shall see whether we can bring the two views into one
conversation at a later point. I want, then, to begin by
talking about talking, as I understand it, helped or hindered as I am by another way of doing philosophy, and
then see what I can do with Mr. Ott's problem from this
angle. This may not help Mr. Ott, especially if he wants
to continue to do philosophy in his way and not in mine,
but if I could gain a bit of clarity for myself, perhaps the
effort will not have been completely in vain.

Let me begin by suggesting that one of the most important distinguishing characteristics of man is that he
speaks. He uses words. He does other things as well, but
if you try to imagine what human life would be like without language, it would come out as something very different from what we know as human life. If you imagined
even a different language, one, for example, which had no
past tense or future tense, but only the present, it would
already lead to a rather different picture. One of Witt-

genstein's more penetrating remarks, I would say, is that to imagine a language is to imagine a form of life.

Since we can speak, we can also think. I put it that way intentionally, in order to draw your attention to the fact that thinking is something which we could not do, or not do as we now do it, if we knew no words at all. Surely thinking silently is also part of what we mean by living as humans, yet if we changed our language, if we imagined our language to have a different form than it now has, it would seem to follow that our thinking would be of a somewhat different sort. I am not trying to make any great point with this somewhat commonplace observation except to indicate that I do not intend to consider the word "thinking" in our theme as a separate subject. If we could understand our speaking, we should probably understand at least most of our thinking. Whatever problems we have, we know most of them as problems because we cannot seem to say what we mean, or we doubt we mean what we say, and so it is in the realm of speaking and in our use of words that we tend to misunderstand each other and ourselves. If these considerations have no force, then you will simply have to accept the fact that I am going to focus on the problem of speaking, or the problems which arise out of some of the ways in which some of us use some words.

One way to date the rise of modern analytical philosophy is by reference to the point at which its early practitioners recovered from the anti-metaphysical fever from which logical positivism had been suffering for some time. When it was acknowledged, beginning about a quarter of a century ago, that the verification principle was itself a glorious bit of metaphysics, the earlier narrow conception of language had to go. The verification principle, that the meaning of a word is the method of its verification, was seen to be itself unverifiable; it was neither empirical nor analytic, but rather one of those sorts of principles by which a man proposes a way of seeing the world and of saying how things are. This led to the new slogan, "Don't ask for the meaning [i.e., don't ask for the method of verification], ask for the use." Words are something like tools, it was suggested. Learning the meaning of a word is learning how to use it, just as one has to learn how to use a saw or a chisel. As a certain children's book has it, "A Hole is to Dig." If you listen to a child learning new words, you will notice that they learn to make the sound, but then they have to learn how to use the word the way the rest of us do. Sometimes they have it right, and sometimes they don't. With practice and some correction from their elders, they learn to use it correctly; that is, they learn its meaning; though how it is we come to recognize what we call the correct use of a word is itself a most interesting question, a question, I would suggest, not completely unlike the more elaborate process by which we establish the attribution of a painting that has been but recently discovered.

We all use words. Some people use them in the business of making steel. Others, or the same people in another context, use them in making love. How different are the uses of the word "making" in these two cases! To illustrate quite another difference, a ball is used in one way in tennis and in another in baseball. To assume that words always behave the same way, so that we could find the meaning by means of definition, once and for all, would lead us to a confusion similar to that which would result from trying to catch a tennis serve and put our opponent out. It has been suggested that language be thought of as something to be found in the context of a game, and that words make sense, if they do, precisely in the context of the game in which they are used. It is well that we keep the context in mind, but even more important is the relationship, if I may put it that way, between language and language-users. For if I say something with passion, it is not quite the same thing as when I say the same words ironically. And the varieties of ways in which I can say the same words, the different ways in which I can associate myself with my words, the varieties of personal investment which my words may carry, all have a great deal to do with what I mean when I say something, and what I am taken to mean by the person or persons to whom I am speaking. Indeed, this business of talking to one another is a most complex and curious business.

I have said nothing of the other things we do, which sometimes accompany and sometimes replace our words: gestures of various sorts, a raised eyebrow, a whistle, a studied silence, a shrug of the shoulder. If we are talking about talking, we should also bear in mind that there are limits to talking. We communicate with one another in more than verbal ways, even if these other ways would be quite different had we no words at all. To imagine gesture (or thinking) as it might be in a world without any knowledge of words is surely to imagine a form of life so different from any we know that words fail us to describe it—which is just the point.

There is a limit to language in another sense. Some of the things that matter most to us are the hardest of which to speak. It would not be difficult for me to describe my fountain pen to you. It would be very difficult for me to describe my closest friend to you. If I lost my pen, I could tell you what to look for with some hope that my description would help. If I were to describe my closest friend's face to you, I am not at all sure you would be able to recognize him. I think I could recognize him in a crowd of a thousand faces right now, but I find it very puzzling to tell you how I could do so. Recognizing a face is also not unlike recognizing the right use of a word. Because we have such difficulties in speaking of some of the most ordinary but important things, we also have poets. I suppose that if Hölderlin is Mr. Ott's poet, then mine would be W. H. Auden, and in writing this paper I have had in mind his words written as notes for an unwritten poem:

" 'My Love,' says the poet, 'is more wonderful, more beautiful, more to be desired than . . .'—there follows a list of admirable natural objects and human artifacts— (*more wonderful,* I should like to say, *than Swaledale or the coast of North-West Iceland, more beautiful than a badger, a sea-horse or a turbin built by Gilkes & Co. of Kendal, more to be desired than cold toast for breakfast or unlimited hot water. . . .*)

"What do such comparisons provide? Certainly not a description by which *you* could be distinguished from a hundred possible rivals of a similar type.

" 'The One I worship has more soul than other folks. . . .' (*Much funnier,* I should like to say.) To be accurate, should not the poet have written . . . 'than any I have met so far'?

" 'I will love You for ever,' swears the poet. I find this easy to swear too. *I will love You at 4.15 p.m. next Tuesday:* is that still as easy? " 'I will love You whatever happens, even though . . .'—there follows a list of catastrophic miracles—(*even though,* I should like to say, *all the stones of Baalbek split into exact quarters, the rooks of Repton utter dire prophecies in Greek and the Windrush bellow imprecations in Hebrew, Time run boustrophedon and Paris and Vienna thrice be lit again by gas. . . .*)

"Do I believe that these events might conceivably occur during my lifetime? If not, what have I promised? *I will love you whatever happens, even though you put on twenty pounds or become afflicted with a moustache:* dare I promise that?

"This poem I wished to write was to have expressed exactly what I mean when I think the words *I love You,* but

88

I cannot exactly know what I mean; it was to have been self-evidently true, but words cannot verify themselves. So this poem will remain unwritten."[1]

Although I seem to have wandered away from the field of combat, my meandering has not been without guile, for I have been trying to lead you astray, it may be, or into another way of thinking about language which has much to commend it on commonsense grounds and which has also much to contribute to the dissolution of the self-made problems of theologians who are less than fastidious about their use of words. So now let me return to the attack—or perhaps it will turn out to be only a feint.

What is it, according to Mr. Ott, to "objectify"? What is "objectifying speaking"? It is, we are told, to be distant, as opposed to (being whatever it is that one is when one is) speaking as a friend and from within a friendship. (100) I think I can understand that. I can speak about a person with some detachment, objectively, we would say. But if the person were my close friend, and I were engaged in intimate conversation with him, my words would be different and my personal investment in my words would be of a different sort. There does not seem to be any problem here. There is not even a problem, or one that I can see, when we move into the realm of theology. A theologian may speak rather objectively of Schleiermarcher's or Barth's conception of Jesus Christ, and when he does so, he will be discussing their words. His speaking will be, as it were, a second-order undertaking, a talking about talking. But if he happened to be a believer and as a believer were to make a confession of faith, he would probably speak in a different way. I do not find this either puzzling or a problem.

We are further told by Mr. Ott that "to reduce all legitimate theological reflection about the text in question to the pure establishing of its claim" would be "an objectifying abstraction that does not correspond to the true nature of thinking and language." (104) I shall not deny that there is a problem here, namely the problem of making sense of this passage. I hope I am not missing Mr. Ott's point entirely if I try to analyze this passage and begin by cutting it to its constituent parts as follows: to reduce thinking—in this case, the thinking of a theologian about a biblical text—to reduce thinking to the establishing of a claim . . . but here I must stop already. Does "the establishing of a claim" mean "making good a claim"? How else is a claim established? If I try to imagine situations in which someone might use the phrase, "establishing a claim," I am led to imagine some sort of act whereby a claim is turned into a possession. I imagine a pioneer staking out a claim, and then years later, returning to establish his claim by the act of settling on it, farming it, and the like. Or I can imagine the government establishing its claim to my service by the action of drafting me into the army. But notice that in each case, the person or agency which makes the claim is the only one who can establish it. Others may recognize the claim or even guarantee the claim, in certain cases, but establishing a claim is an act, an act of the one making the claim.

This, it seems to me, is the meaning, the use, of this expression.

In order to make any sense out of the passage before us, however, I must at least rearrange it to read: to reduce theological reflection to pointing out that a given biblical text was written by someone who wanted to make a claim, or who was saying that someone else had a claim upon the reader, is to make an abstraction of some sort. That is admittedly a narrow way to think about a text, and my rearrangement would make some sense of the word "reduce," but why should this one-track way of thinking lead to an abstraction, objectifying or otherwise? This seems an odd thing to say. On the other hand, if I make room for the word "abstraction," then I must leave the passage as it was published, and that leaves me wondering what to make of the verb "reduce." I don't know what it means to "reduce thinking," least of all into an action. Since the translation appears to be correct, Mr. Ott seems to have used the wrong verb. Let me clarify this.

To move from thought to action is not inconceivable. We can readily imagine cases in which we could understand such a movement. I think, for example, of the person I love, and I am then moved, we should say, to write that person a letter or to go see them. There is a certain logic to this, but I see no hope of introducing anything but confusion by calling this movement one of reduction. Just what word to use here depends on the thought and the action involved, of course, so I leave it to Mr. Ott to make his own correction. As the passage stands, it is a muddle, not a mystery.

Second, whatever sort of movement it is that stands between thought and action, it is certainly not an abstraction in any usual sense of that word. We might want to call it a consequence (speaking ethically, not logically), or we might want to call it a mistake. But an abstraction, objective or nonobjective, is hardly an understandable thing to say of this movement.

In sum, either this passage consists of one great mass of confusions arising from a most inexact use of words, or else I have completely missed the author's point. But if this last is true, then I believe that I have shown grounds for saying that whatever it was that Mr. Ott wanted to say, he did not in fact say it. I am left with the question, then, what did he want to say, and why did he not say what he meant? The answer to these questions might help us get at that peculiar word, objectifying, which he has used here.

I turn to another use of this confusing word. Objectifying, I am told, is one of those things which metaphysics does, or if I may correct this, since metaphysics is what people do, he who does metaphysics thereby objectifies. (107) Such I take to be a more or less correct translation of what Mr. Ott meant to say. Now how does this come about? The answer we are given is this: "It thinks them (i.e., beings) as beings by formulating them in concepts." Again, having never met a "metaphysics" that went about thinking, I translate this to read: When a man is doing metaphysics, he thinks of beings by means of concepts. Now this assertion is by no means clear to me, for I am puzzled by Mr. Ott's conception of metaphysics, and I am not sure just what he means with the term "concepts." Surely I am engaged in metaphysics whenever I say how things are, for is it not of the nature of doing metaphysics that rather than attempting to give us new information about the world, the one so engaged is proposing a way in which to conceive or picture or think about all the information which we have already? One way of doing metaphysics is met by Mr. Ott's assertion, but that is only true insofar as it is granted that Mr. Ott is engaged in a metaphysical task himself. He proposes to us another metaphysics. If I say that love is real, or that to lose myself is truly to find myself, am I not also making metaphysical claims, or is there not at least a metaphysical underpinning to these assertions?

It seems evident, however, that Mr. Ott wants to reserve the word "metaphysics" for one kind of metaphysics, and that is perfectly allowable so long as we are all aware of what is going on. But now let me ask further, if I think of the one I love (whom I hope Mr. Ott will allow to be a being, but I am now so uncertain of what he is saying that I am not even sure of this), do I do so with the use of concepts? Well, it does depend on how he means the word "concept." Apparently he wants to say that there is a way in which I can think of my beloved which is "objectifying" and another way which is not. If I move this to the level of speaking, I suppose this means

93

that I can talk *about my beloved, as one human being among others, and I can talk to* my beloved, as "the only one for me," and if that is all that is being said, there is again no problem.

This interpretation is confirmed as Mr. Ott goes on to lump together with metaphysics the way a scientist thinks and the way a technologist thinks. I would very much doubt that it is anywhere near so obviously the case as Mr. Ott thinks that any scientist "assumes there are facts which he can establish just as they are by means of his capacity to think."(108) I doubt that many scientists would recognize themselves in this picture any more than many metaphysicians would, although I certainly do not want to put it beyond the bounds of possibility that Mr. Ott may have once met a metaphysician who saw the world in this way. Not having met such a man, I am inclined to regard him as a hypothetical figure who, for the purposes of our discussion, is really a "straw man."

In spite of my difficulties in making sense of these various passages in which the word "objectifying" appears, I nonetheless think that I have gained at least a general sense of where Mr. Ott is going and what he is about. I get the impression that he wants to encourage us to think of doing theology as if it were a kind of immediate response, in which there is no nasty conceptualizing ("anthropological-sociological conceptualizing" he calls it, borrowing from Heidegger, and presumably—and, from my point of view, unhappily—meaning these as bad words), a response of the sort, I imagine, which the lover might make upon meeting his beloved. This conception of theologizing, it seems to me, is not far removed from what most people would call "believing" or faith, or from what Schleiermacher called "religion." If this is the case (and Mr. Ogden pointed this out in his published response), then when Mr. Ott asks for theology to be a non-objectifying kind of thinking, he is coming close to identifying the doing of theology with believing. In which case, I assume that proper theological writing, in Mr. Ott's judgment, should take the form of prayer, as in Anselm's *Proslogion*, or in parts of it. That would seem to rule out of theological court any critical reflection on Anselm's undertaking, not to speak of other writings of Anselm, such as his *Cur Deus Homo,* which I had always taken to be a theological production. And this conception of theology would also seem to entail the judgment that even the *Proslogion* is proper theology only insofar as it avoids the use of concepts. To all this I can only say that this is undoubtedly one way of conceiving the theological task, although it does not seem to be the one displayed by Mr. Ott's essay. How could it, for is not prayer essentially private, and can it find place for argumentation?

The nature of my argument, if such it be, precludes my challenging Mr. Ott's conception of theology in any other way than by offering an alternative way of doing theology. I shall introduce this other way by raising a question about the model of poetry which Mr. Ott finds so appealing, although I shall shift the model in so doing. I certainly do not wish to deny that it is possible to think of

95

a poet as having one great unspoken and unspeakable poem within him, as it were, of which each of his actual poems is only an imperfect manifestation. This way of thinking is as old and as venerable as its great champion Plato. Now, to shift the model so as to give us a fresh start, it is again possible to imagine a painter as having one great picture in his mind, as it were, and of each of his actual paintings as only an imperfect manifestation or reflection of this ideal. Indeed, if we do not notice how attractive is this way of thinking, this image that has captivated Mr. Ott and many another from Plato on, we shall never treat it with adequate respect and it will return to haunt us again and again.

Consider the paintings of Cézanne. Is there not something, indeed a good deal, that might tempt us to say that Cézanne spent his life trying to paint that picture which plagued him and which he could never reproduce satisfactorily? Did he not spend literally as much as twenty minutes staring ahead of him between single brushstrokes, and did he not say that he could never *"réaliser"* what he was after? Did he not paint the same picture, or rather the same subject, again and again, never satisfied with the results? Yes, the Platonic model is attractive. But let us not forget some other facts. One man, and so far as I am aware, only one man ever interpreted Cézanne's work in this way, and that was his old friend Émile Zola. And when Zola's interpretation was published, Cézanne was so furious with the suggestion that he was forever trying in vain to actualize an ideal painting that he broke off the relationship with Zola for good. And there is the further fact that no reputable art historian or critic has ever attempted to use Zola's model of thought as a way to interpret Cézanne's work.

Suppose, now, that you discovered a painting in your attic which you thought might possibly be an unknown Cézanne. What would have led you to this suspicion? Something about the brushwork? The odd distortion that marks so many of Cézanne's works? The peculiar effect of a painting that seems to have been painted from several points in succession, so that the perspective is multiple, not unified? Yet each painting of his is different and his style changed radically at several points in his career. Do we ask whether this seems to be another attempted realization of that one unpaintable Cézannesque ideal, or do we not, rather, compare it with each of the paintings that are known? Do we not ask the advice of those who have studied these different paintings with great care, who are respected as experts on Cézanne, who might then conclude, if we were lucky, that indeed this must be an unknown Cézanne, although it reveals a new element in his development not hitherto noticed with much care. I suggest that in fact we would follow some such practice, and I fail to see that anything has been lost by foregoing the image of an ideal Cézanne picture. Nor, might I add, do we lose anything of substance if we forego an image of the ideal or one true Gospel, but that is something to which I wish to return later.

Let us turn from the image of an ideal painting or the

poet's one unspoken poem or the one true Gospel and look at what lies before us. Christians have always had to take what lies before them with some seriousness, and why not? They believe, they have faith. Let us begin there and see what happens, and I see no reason to be ashamed that greater men than any of us, supremely Schleiermacher, have begun at this point, as they understood it.

Believers, or some of them, are as men who are in love, and because they are in love, they speak. They may speak to their beloved, or to what they take to be their beloved, or to their own image of their beloved. They also speak, no doubt, to each other, in order to share their love or their awareness of this love. I suppose this language is what Mr. Ott would call non-objectifying language, the language with which men say such things as "Thou are the Christ," and "I know that my Redeemer liveth," and also "Depart from me Lord, for I am sinful man." But these words sound as if they were spoken to someone, and I fail to see that it would be objectionable for a man who spoke in this way to say, "Let me tell you about the object of my love." May not the language of love refer at times to the *object* of love, and may not the language of faith refer at times to the beloved or awful *object* of faith? In the ordinary sense and use of these words, I fail to see that anything illegitimate or even inappropriate is going on here.

But even at this point it should be noted that the lover makes his declaration of love in a certain context. He may have read or heard other declarations or poems of love. As a creature of time and space even his most basic utterances will reflect his context in history. The believer as well as the lover as well as the poet stands in a certain cultural framework, and insofar as his immediate response steps beyond utter privacy in the smallest degree, that framework will manifest itself.

Let us bring the language of the lover and the language of the believer closer together by pushing further. Suppose that the object of a man's love is no longer with him. Suppose his beloved has gone far away, or has died, to make the point clearer. What now is the object of his love? Certainly it is not an empirically discoverable person, as was the case before. Maybe his love now takes the form of a profound dedication to do the things which he understood his beloved wanted, or the things which he imagines his beloved would want if he or she were still alive and present. Maybe he would tell stories about his beloved, in order that he may keep the image alive. Maybe the image is so alive for him that, if he conceives of the world in a certain way, he may actually think that his beloved *is* alive, in some extended and not very precise use of the word.

Someone might say, "He is not in love with his dead beloved—he is in love with his own memory of her." Perhaps so, but I am not at all clear what the difference is, and therefore I am not at all sure that any point is being made. Doesn't being in love with a departed loved-one mean to love one's memory of that person?

99

It may be, if I may just touch on another point, that if you honor the memory of your departed grandfather, you will seek to learn all you can about him from other sources, a sort of quest, we might call it, of the historical grandfather. But if the results of the quest are negative or if the evidence runs counter to the memory, it will probably take a very long time before those results will be accepted, and when they are, they will be assimilated to the memory and made a part of it, so that the image will remain an image in the memory. Is it not odd that fond memory leads us to want to know how it actually was with the one we say we remember, yet we cannot allow anything so learned to change the memory in any serious way? In a peculiar way, fond memory both stirs historical curiosity and refuses historical refutation, which means that fond memory's historical curiosity is highly uncritical. We might conclude from this that, in the last analysis, memory really has no deep interest in the past, and that a faith which claims to be grounded in historical events is actually not interested in historical investigation. Yet why do our ears perk up when we hear someone speak of our grandfathers? But that is another and most complex problem and we have difficulties enough on our hands with our assigned subject.

Let us now add a further development: Among several persons who share the same object of love, that is, who say that the beloved they remember is the same one, among them there arises a disagreement about whether a certain course of action is appropriate to those who loved

this one. Or maybe they disagree over the appropriate-
ness of speaking of their beloved in a certain way: is he
like the most wonderful thing you can imagine, or is he
really one and the same thing with the greatest thing that
you can imagine? They check their memories; they discuss; each tries to make the most persuasive case that he
can for his conclusions, his way of seeing the matter, his
way of speaking. Behold, of such is theology, a second-
order activity arising out of the first-order activity of believers, a talking about the talking of believers. Theology
is language about language, although frequently the language it is about is language jammed hard up against its
limits.

How do theological arguments arise? Sometimes they
arise out of historical inaccuracies and misinterpreta-
tions of texts and the like. Primarily, however, they arise
out of the limits of language about areas of experience
which seem to elude precise and systematic linguistic expression; not, I would suggest, out of a conflict between
nonconceptual thinking and speaking and some other
way of speaking and thinking, call it abstract, or con-
ceptual, or objectifying or "distant."

How do we settle theological arguments? Well, how do
we decide about the attribution of a newly discovered
painting? How do we decide whether the sonnets attributed to Shakespeare and the sonnets attributed to
Edward De Vere are by the same poet? Indeed, how do
we decide whether someone is using a word correctly? It
is, in reply to this last, a shortcut which hides what is

going on if we answer, "Go look up the word in the dictionary." Argument by definition is as useless as argument by derivation. For how do we agree on what is a dictionary, and how are dictionaries made in the first place? Or even more important, how are dictionaries changed, revised and brought up-to-date, as we say?

It may not be the whole truth, but there is surely much truth in the conception of language as a convention established among its users, and also of language as a set of tools which we have learned how to use from those who fashioned them before us for certain uses. And the attribution of a painting is also a matter of consensus, of comparing and arguing and of calling in the experts. The experts can always be proved wrong, of course, but until they are, they remain what we agree to call experts.

How, then, do we identify the Gospel? To ask the question that way is already to slide into that model of thought which I wish at least to bracket by suggesting that there are other ways of looking at the matter. It is to allow that ghost to haunt us which I have been trying to lay. Let us ask instead what Paul means—not means, but meant—when he said what he did to the people in Corinth, and let us ask what we might take them to have taken Paul to mean. There is Paul's meaning, and there may have been more than one Corinthian meaning. And then we can begin to add other meanings: what the document called I Corinthians meant to an Athanasius or a Jerome, what it meant to a Thomas or a Calvin. And there still remains what this document means to a contemporary preacher, how he uses it, what he thinks he sees in it. And, of course, there are also the ways in which his words are taken by his hearers. Between all these uses of the same collection of words, words being repeated in many different contexts and by many different people, it may be possible and instructive to trace certain formal similarities and maybe even what we would take to be certain substantive similarities. Much theologizing consists in arguing the force of certain similarities, as over against others or as over against dissimilarities. But theologians, in this way in which I am thinking, would be chasing after a will-o'-the-wisp, after a figment of their imagination, if they sought in all this *The* Gospel. Theologians would be better occupied in exploring the various uses which present themselves in the contemporary language of believers, undertaking a functional, or logical, and critical analysis of the various possible uses arising in discussions about the possible meanings of I Corinthians or any other document, biblical or otherwise, which believers choose to discuss. Their task lies in a running discussion and a running clarification of the alternatives offered and their various implications, not only among themselves, I would add, as we are doing here, but also with any believers who are willing to listen, so that the various merits and demerits of these various meanings or uses of the language of believers may become clear.

Is *The* Gospel lying, as it were, behind all particular Gospels and coming to partial expression in them? This question, Mr. Ott seems to think, is not unlike the question of there being one poem lying behind all the particular poems which a poet actually writes, a great unspoken poem which is never fully realized in any of his actual poems, nor in all of them together. The question I ask in return is this: does the model of one ideal painting help or hinder our appreciation and understanding of Cézanne's actual paintings? Conversely, does the model of one eternal Gospel help us to read and understand the particular and diverse materials in the New Testament and even more diverse materials of contemporary religious and theological writings? The model of *The* Gospel is one way, one way among others, to look at the New testament and the history of Christian thought, and discussion over whether there is such a thing as *The* Gospel is a discussion over the merits and demerits of this way of looking at those documents and that history. And if someone were to write a book and call it something like *The Secular Meaning of the Gospel,* his book should not be misunderstood as having been anything more—and what more could it ever have been?—than an invitation (as is every metaphysical undertaking) to look at the matter in question in a certain way, or as one suggestion about how to talk about certain limits to language arising in certain circumstances.

Mr. Ott has his way of looking at the theological task. Doing theology, for Mr. Ott, is possibly related to praying. The alternative suggested is another way of doing theology, much more akin to doing logical analysis, literary criticism and art history. Yes, and it is even akin to doing sociology and anthropology. One merit of this alternative cannot resist pointing out. It has no problem at all with objectifying language.

N O T E S

[1] W. H. Auden, *Homage to Clio*, London, Faber & Faber, Ltd., 1958, pp. 50-51.

VI

❧

Bonhoeffer's Paradox:
Living With God Without God

A Hypothetical Investigation

WHEN PEOPLE SAY THINGS OF AN ILLOGICAL SORT, WHEN they combine contradictory elements in one sentence, we often dismiss them as muddled or stupid. There are cases, however, in which we are inclined to treat illogicalities with more respect, cases in which something about the person, the way he speaks or the situation leads us to suspect that the illogicality, the paradox, is intentional. Intentional paradoxes are sometimes signals of a discovery, a discovery of a new way of seeing something all too familiar. Some intentional paradoxes serve to shake us loose from old mental habits and lead us to the point at which the speaker stands, from which we may see things in his new way. They invite us to share in a newly discovered view of familiar matters.

I want to explore Dietrich Bonhoeffer's paradoxical language about God in order to see if it is of this sort. If we assume that he was not stupid or talking nonsense, then we shall proceed under the assumption that he may have had something important to say with his paradox, that he may have had a new way of seeing things, or at least a way of seeing things that was new for him. This presumed discovery of Bonhoeffer's, then, shall be our goal, which means that we are looking for a clear view of the way in which Bonhoeffer was looking at things. Our method will be to go behind his parodox, as it were, in order to work through his discovery without feeling obliged to leave it in the words in which he left it—that is, as a paradox. What I shall argue is that his paradox signals a shift in world hypothesis, in root metaphors for understanding life and the world, in short, in metaphysics. Bonhoeffer intended to reject one world hypothesis, one metaphysics. From the fragments remaining from the period in which he developed the paradox which we are to investigate, it is not altogether clear whether he thought, as have so many other theologians, that he was thereby free from involvement in any metaphysics. I think he thought that he was, for there is no evidence that he was aware that to reject one view of things is already to have adopted another view. It is this displacement of hypotheses that seems to me to be the heart of our subject, which is why I have subtitled this paper, "A hypothetical investigation."[1]

The fascinating thing about Bonhoeffer, for many of us in the next generation following him, is that where his theology becomes really interesting, it is preserved in only bits and snatches. One result of this sketchy character of his last ideas is that he has been claimed by the most orthodox and the most radical elements of contemporary theology. The paradox which I have chosen comes from this last period, and indeed, you can dismiss it altogether if you want to. On the one hand, it can be discounted as the uncertain, wild talk of a man who less than a year earlier wrote that he was enjoying reading nontheological authors, as though this were quite a new experience for him. Karl Barth discounted Bonhoeffer's last writings in just this way, seeing in them the expression of the trauma of a man who in prison found himself for the first time in his life outside of the relatively narrow context of church and theology in which he had always lived and thought.

One could also discount our parodox on other grounds. It occurs most clearly in a letter dated July 14, 1944, just six days before the attempt on Hitler's life, the failure of which led to Bonhoeffer's own death. Loose and irresponsible language might be expected in such a time of tension. So who is right, the conservatives or the radicals? God knows what Bonhoeffer meant, that is, what he would have said had he lived to develop his ideas or to see what others found themselves saying because of what he wrote. And to that we may add, God knows what we mean when we use that all-too-common expression, "God knows."

In any case, judging Barth to have been guilty of the genetic fallacy, I do not chose to dismiss Bonhoeffer's parodox. At least I want to think a bit about it. So first of all, let us state it in his words: "*Vor und mit Gott leben wir ohne Gott.*" He put it in other words, too, but this form will do, for, in any case, I want to put the paradox in English, and that in more ways than one. That is to say, I am not primarily interested in Bonhoeffer, but in his paradox, and I mean to investigate it in my way, not his. Literally, the paradox translates, "Before [as it were, in the face of or in the presence of] and with God we live without God." Or, to bring out the paradox a bit more sharply, "We live with God without God," as I put it in my title.

Now when I said I wanted to put that into English, I

intended more than just a verbal translation. I meant that I wanted to explore this paradox as it would be explored in English, which calls for methods of analysis of which Bonhoeffer, as far as I can see, was quite unaware. I mean I want to know what it means, and that means several things. It can mean, I want to see if there is another way of saying the same thing which would not be so liable to draw a blank stare. Or, if "saying the same thing in other words" strikes you as being as problematic and ambiguous an enterprise as it does me, then let us say that I want to see if there is a way to speak that will do for me what this paradoxical sentence in German seems to have done for Bonhoeffer, or at least something related to that. Intellectual honesty, for which Bonhoeffer was also concerned, compels me to say that I cannot hope for more than that. Any way in which we deal with Bonhoeffer's words, or indeed with any other words, involves more or less abstraction. Those words were his, written out of a certain life and in most particular circumstances. Let them stand as they are, part of his own life, speaking for themselves. But we can now proceed to explore our own English paradox which we have abstracted from Bonhoeffer's writings, attempting to set them into our own living context to see how they might come alive. I want to explore this paradox because I think that by doing so, we can shed a bit of light on some of our problems in theology today. I hope to make clear that in that light, we may be seen to be heading in a direction which was reasonably clearly seen by an American thinker some sixty years ago, an American theologian insufficiently appreciated by most of the theological community, namely, William James. And now to our investigation.

The parodox has two sides, "with God" and "without God." Let me begin with the second or negative part first. And here we run into a problem before we can even begin, for Bonhoeffer's point here is not just negative. The negative is enclosed as it were in a positive: living. "Living without God" is the subject, and that involves first of all living. It seems to have meant at least that we are asked to do what we seem to be required by our circumstances to do in any case: to take full responsibility, unqualified responsibility, for working things out on our own, that is, in human terms. This is the positive side of Bonhoeffer's repeated thesis that men do not need God today, that we can and do get along just as well or better without "the God hypothesis" as with it. We cope with life and this world as human beings without recourse to any higher power, some *Deus ex machina*, to help us solve our problems. We may or may not do well, but in any case it is up to us. We do the best we can with what we have at hand: ourselves. The terms of our problems, of our solutions, and of our failures are our own human terms.

But what are human terms? What is it, for Bonhoeffer, to be a man? Clearly the image of man for him was his image of Jesus Christ. To take full responsibility for this world and to work things out in human terms, as Bonhoeffer saw it, was to work things out in terms of the man

Jesus, as Bonhoeffer saw that man. In short, the criterion of manhood was that presented in the biblical story, the story of the despised and rejected "man-for-others." That seems to have been Bonhoeffer's frame of reference. Human terms, did I say? Are there not other than human terms of reference in that story? Does that story not tell us of God? Well, it does in a way, but I gather that Bonhoeffer wanted to emphasize that whatever that story tells us of God, it does so in the human terms provided by the human figure of Jesus Christ. To experience God, he wrote, means to meet Jesus Christ. To be in a relationship to God means to live for others, sharing in that form of life which was Jesus Christ's.

We have, as you see, already passed to the positive side of the paradox, which seems to suggest that we have on our hands only an apparent paradox. For to live with God, "vor und mit Gott," is, as we have said already, to meet Jesus Christ, to live a new life of "being-for-others." Again, the frame of reference is the same: the biblical story of "the man-for-others."

So far, so good, and no doubt everyone may find comfort from this, fit it into his own theological scheme, and find Bonhoeffer on his side. The difficult problems are not yet exposed. So now we dig deeper, carry the analysis a step farther. It was, apparently, an important point for Bonhoeffer that Christian faith did not commit one to what he called repeatedly "the God hypothesis." Indeed, he seems to have almost wanted to say that the Christian should reject the God hypothesis. What was this that he wanted to reject, or that he at least thought was superfluous to Christian faith?

Well, in its broadest terms, the God hypothesis was the theism of Western thought, the theism, for example, of Descartes. And what is wrong with the theism of Descartes? Well, perhaps we could say that Descartes' God is too big. And let us not pretend that Descartes stood alone. The God of Descartes, and not only of Descartes, was the God who could do anything, literally do anything in or about this world. He was unambiguously omnipotent. He was prime mover, first cause, the ground of all being, and all the rest. If he wanted to make us think that every square had three sides and led us to count the sides in such a way that we came up with four every time, he could do that, too. He was the Absolute in all its glory, the Supreme Being raised to the nth degree. In Descartes' terms, Bonhoeffer was an atheist.

Bonhoeffer, I need hardly say, had a God, but it was not the God of Descartes. Bonhoeffer's God was powerful, but it was that odd sort of power that takes the form of weakness. Was he powerful? Well, we find our paradox coming back again, for God's power, according to Bonhoeffer, was in fact the power of powerlessness. He was a weak God, and that is exactly what Bonhoeffer liked about him. We need not state it quite so paradoxically. We may simply say that this God was not omnipotent in any traditional Western sense of the term, and that Bonhoeffer thought there was much to be said for what weakness could accomplish in this world. More questions

115

about this God could be asked, but let us look at the other side of the matter first.

To believe in and rely upon the God of Western theism is to rely on the God hypothesis. Maybe that is not precisely what Bonhoeffer was saying, but let us leave it at that for the moment in order to consider another side of the matter. What sort of hypothesis is this, this God hypothesis? I want to set aside precise questions about this God for the moment and consider hypotheses, opening up this question from a particular angle.

We have many sorts of hypotheses with which we operate. Indeed without hypotheses of a good number of sorts, we could not operate at all. Many of our hypotheses are vague and general, such as the sort we hardly ever formulate for ourselves. We operate on the vague hypotheses that other things being equal, the world we know will go on operating in more or less the same way tomorrow as it did yesterday, that the language we used yesterday will serve us today, that the bread we buy today we shall be able to eat tomorrow. We also have more specific but more restricted hypotheses. We have hypotheses about the flow and distribution of money on which we rely in monetary affairs. We have hypotheses of yet more exact form on which we rely in scientific work. We call these hypotheses, because, although we rely on them, we also test them out by our further experience. We rely on them insofar as they seem to check out, insofar as they serve their purpose and allow us to proceed without confusion or chaos, insofar as with their help we find that we can move through life.

There is also another sort of hypothesis with which we operate, which may be vague for one and specific for another. Insofar as the world we experience, the world of money, politics, science and all the rest, insofar as this is all part of the world we experience, we tend to see this world in one way or another. We have, each of us, whether precise or fuzzy, whether explicit or implicit, a view of the world. There comes a point for any of us at which we find we want to say, "But this is how things are. They just are this way." And if we take the trouble to become aware and articulate about our world views, and if we then attempt to say what they are, what we are doing may also be called metaphysics.

What is metaphysics? Well, the most general answer, I suppose, would be that it is an attempt to describe the structure of our understanding of how things are generally, that is, how the whole is, how everything taken together is. Or to put it in other words, it is an attempt to describe the workings of the language in which we say "this is how things are." I say "describe," but I do not wish to pretend that metaphysicians merely describe what is already seen by all. In a sense, of course, this is exactly what they do, for every metaphysics has been a particular proposal of a way of seeing and therefore of talking about what is before us all the time. But it is also a proposal. Any one metaphysics bids for our agreement, not always there before we hear the proposal, that things are like this, not that. In describing what may be called the structure of our understanding of the world, or what I should prefer to call our way of speaking of the world, a metaphysical system or hypothesis is offering us a particular description which we are asked to accept, and this may call on us to revise our familiar descriptions. In this sense, I should be cautious about drawing a hard and fast line between revisionary and descriptive metaphysics.

A metaphysics is by its character a hypothesis. That is, it is proposed to us as a way to see the world, a way to speak of the world, and the assumption seems to be that we shall find that this checks out with our own experience of the world. Since it is, in one way of defining it, a description or an attempted description of the structure of our understanding of the universe, since it appeals to our understanding, bids to be the key to our understanding, a dogmatic metaphysics is a self-contradiction. Metaphysics is by its own proper role hypothetical, asking to be tested, subject to revision on the basis of further experience. It entails at its heart the critical role of understanding.

Now we take a difficult step: I want to argue at this point that Christian faith, in its traditional forms and expressions has been, or, if you prefer, has implied, a world view of just this sort. That is to say, the believer has found himself at certain points forced to say, "But this is how things are." Moreover, he has had to say this concerning matters central to his understanding of things as a believer. Indeed, it is at just these points, although not only here, of course, that he has spoken of God. Taking metaphysics as I have, as it has been understood increasingly since the revolution through which English-speaking philosophy passed during the second quarter of this century, as an exposition of a way of seeing what is before us all the time, the whole world of our experience, I do not see how we could deny that every Christian theology is in its broad lines a particular metaphysics. It has a view of the whole, of heaven and earth, it has a root metaphor, of a personal God and his creation, and it bids for or assumes our agreement that this is indeed how things are. Not only do I fail to see how one can deny this; I see no reason whatsoever for any theologian wanting to deny this. A so-called Biblical Theology, of the sort that was in high fashion in the forties and fifties, for example, may wish to have no part of the particular metaphysics of Aristotle or of Plato, or of Descartes for that matter. Of course not, for these are other metaphysics, in competition with the way of saying how things are which was characteristic of that particular twentieth-century metaphysics called Biblical Theology.

If this view of theology is allowed, if in this contemporary sense it is recognized that a theology is one sort of metaphysics, then it is, as we have argued, a hypothesis. It may be a hypothesis held with profound conviction and great dedication, but it is a hypothesis nonetheless. Its proponent asks us to test and see, even to taste and see whether the world is not as it depicts it. It bids us to test and to think, and when it takes a dogmatic turn (using the word in its pejorative sense), when it rules out the critical role of understanding, it breaks with its own tradition of faith seeking understanding, it turns from the

Logos it claims to detect and worship, it becomes something contrary to man rather than for man. In this sense, theology as metaphysics is hypothetical, open to correction, subject to further reflection, criticism and revision.

If one reflects on the general form of theology as a world hypothesis, as a metaphysics, it is evident that God has been not only a piece of this hypothesis, as theology has on the whole developed in the West. God has been the key figure, and that in a particular way. In any metaphysics, one comes sooner or later to the element or elements which are sometimes called first principles. You can find out which they are by asking, what must I be able to talk about, in this view of things, in order to talk about the other things? I think I am being reasonably fair to most Western theology, at least up until modern times, if I say that it has been argued that in order to understand, to talk about man and the world, one must be able to speak of God. That is to say, one speaks of man or the world in terms of, or in their relations to God. Man and the world are God" creatures, and unless we begin speaking of man and the world in that way, the tradition argued, all our further speaking will be false. This is what is involved in saying that in traditional Western theology, God has had ontological priority, or God has been the unique first principle, whether in the theology of Aquinas or in that of Calvin. It means that God is the term of reference for everything else, that we speak of man and the world in reference to God, not the reverse. As a result, speaking of God was in no sense a secondary problem for traditional theology, by no means a problem to be turned over to apologetics or practical theology. On the contrary, for the Western tradition, speaking of God was, we may say, of the very essence of the theological enterprise. Theology was what its name can be read to mean etymologically: language about God, from beginning to end.

By this line of argument, we find traditional theology to be a metaphysics, a world hypothesis in which God is the single first principle, having linguistic or ontological priority. It is not misleading, therefore, to speak of this as a God-hypothesis. It is a hypothesis about everything that is, and the central term, logically and linguistically, is God. If you wish to reject this God-hypothesis, you may do so, but you may then be asked what you propose to put in its place. As a way of considering that, let us see where we come out with Bonhoeffer's theology when looked at in the light of these considerations.

Bonhoeffer argued that Christian faith does not give us a hypothesis for solving many of the problems with which we are faced. Its hypothesis provides no help in dealing, for example, with problems of physics or astronomy or geology, and this goes rather far toward denying to theology the role of a world hypothesis. We do not first need to speak of God in order to speak of these other matters. That means that in at least these regions of discourse, God does not have ontological priority. Yet for Bonhoeffer, in at least some important regions of human life and language, the story of Jesus Christ, Jesus as "the man-for-others," the behavior of Jesus within the biblical story as Bonhoeffer read it, was the key to understanding, the first principle, that which he said we must first be able to speak of before we can properly speak of other matters. If not so surely universal in scope as the God-hypothesis of the tradition, yet within the range of human ethical, political and cultural behavior, a Jesus-hypothesis, or a Christ-hypothesis is operative in Bonhoeffer's view of things. Moreover, what we mean by the word "God" must be learned from how we speak of Jesus. That is to say, we shall not properly speak of God unless we have first learned to speak of Jesus, and we shall then speak of God in terms of Jesus, not the reverse. Jesus, or more strictly, the behavior of Jesus, Jesus as "the man-for-others" now displaces God as the root metaphor, now takes the place of ontological priority.

But, it might be objected, was not this ontological priority of Jesus implicit in the doctrine of the Trinity, at least if we see that doctrine through the eyes of Karl Barth? If the God of Christian faith is unqualifiedly the one who makes himself known in Jesus Christ, then was Bonhoeffer saying anything other than that which Barth had said? And in that case, is this not still a God-hypothesis, specifically the peculiar sort of God-hypothesis of Barth's *Dogmatik*? Then are not Bonhoeffer's disparaging remarks about the God-hypothesis actually misleading? For on this showing, he was arguing not against every God-hypothesis, but only against one and for another. In which case, the conservatives may lay full claim to Bonhoeffer, whereas the radicals would appear to have misled us by appealing to his last writings.

I am not particularly interested in settling the question of who has the better claim to Bonhoeffer credentials, but it does seem to be overdoing it to claim that Bonhoeffer was arguing for a Trinitarian God-hypothesis as simply as this objection concludes. Some important discrepancies have been overlooked. Although it may be said that shifting ontological priority from God to Christ is only a tiny move farther in the direction in which Barth had already taken a theology of revelation, still it is a step farther and an important one. With this little step, although we may continue to speak of God, we are required to speak of God in terms of the first principle, who is, after all, a man. Certainly not "man-in-himself," Bonhoeffer insisted, whatever that may be, but "the man-for-others." Yet for all that, man, specifically a particular man, is now the first principle, the key to understanding even God, and it is in terms of this man that we are to learn how to speak of God. Is this still within the range of Barth's thought? A relationship between the thought of these men is not to be denied, but I should think one could make a better case for setting Bonhoeffer within another realm of discourse, for understanding him in the light of the thought of one who opposed what I think is the same God-hypothesis that Bonhoeffer rejected, the God of rationalism, of classical Western theism, and who did so precisely for the sake of man. William James, almost forty years before

Bonhoeffer, granted that the idea of the omnipotent, absolute God of Western theism had a certain nobility, but
then remarked, in words which I think Bonhoeffer would
rather have enjoyed, had he ever read them: "In this real
world of sweat and dirt, it seems to me that when a view
of things is 'noble,' that ought to count as a presumption
against its truth, and as a philosophic disqualification.
The prince of darkness may be a gentleman, as we are
told he is, but whatever the God of earth and heaven is,
he can surely be no gentleman. His menial services are
needed in the dust of our human trails, even more than
his dignity is needed in the empyrean." James never developed an explicitly christological basis for this way of
speaking of God, yet the affinity is no less interesting.
Formally speaking, the structure of Bonhoeffer's and
James's metaphysics do not seem to be so different. In
each there is serious language about God, and, in each,
man in the sweat and dirt of this real world gives us the
terms for speaking of God. In each, God is weak and man
is called to full responsibility for what is to come of
things. Let me illustrate with one more passage from
James. Speaking of his idea of the world as unfinished, as
growing "piecemeal by the contribution of its several
parts," James wrote: "Take the hypothesis seriously and as
a live one. Suppose that the world's author put the case to
you before creation, saying: 'I am going to make a world
not certain to be saved, a world the perfection of which
shall be conditional merely, the condition being that each
several agent does its own "level best." I offer you the

chance of taking part in such a world. Its safety, you see, is unwarranted. It is a real adventure, with real danger, yet it may win through. It is a social scheme of cooperative work, genuinely to be done. Will you join the procession? Will you trust yourself and trust the other agents enough to face the risk?' " James hoped that we would, for he felt we would see that this is just the world we do in fact live in, a world of risk and danger, in which it matters what we do. Is not this also the risky, dangerous, adventurous world that Bonhoeffer saw, in which God surely fails again and again, in which we gamble on its winning through, but hold no guarantee that it will?

I think I am aware of the ways in which it is silly to think of William James as a theologian. I wish I were as sure that we could agree that it would be simply stupid for us today not to take James seriously in our present attempts to find our way ahead in the theological enterprise. However you may feel about that one, I want to try out the framework on which James was working during his last years, to see how Bonhoeffer's and our problem looks in this new setting. The procedure may be a bit unusual, but the results may be at least entertaining, and possibly even instructive.

What I am suggesting calls upon us to consider the possibilities of the hypothesis of a limited God within a pluralistic universe. Let us take this slowly, a piece at a time. What sort of hypothesis is that of a pluralistic universe: Well, as the word universe warns us, it is a world hypothesis, an all-inclusive view of things. But as a hypothesis of the structure of the totality of our understandings, it says that we understand the whole by understanding the parts. To know the whole better means nothing other than seeing the different parts more and more clearly in the infinite variety of their interconnections and relationships, in their disparities and disjunctions, as well as in their similarities and connections. The world is one, as James liked to put it, insofar forth as conjunctions pertain, but then not one insofar forth as disjunctions pertain. The universe of our understanding, of our experience, or, I should like to add, of our language, may be seen as a cube through which many different lines can be and are drawn, going in every sort of direction. Some of the lines are long, going from one side to another; some are short, suspended in thin air, as it were, not touching any side of the cube. Some lines touch none or few of the other lines, some touch many other lines at many points. And, of course, for any particular purpose which you may have in mind, you can always insert other lines, make or notice other connections, break some of the connections which you have found.

Such is one model of pluralism, a root metaphor of plurality as a hypothesis of how we actually experience, understand, and speak in and of the world. It does not have any one first principle. It has many principles, and which is first and which second depends on what you are trying to do or understand at the moment. Marx gave us some useful first principles which proved to be helpful in certain areas of our experience and with which it turned out to be possible to draw such different lines as Communist ideology and the discipline of sociology. If social analysis is your aim, here are some first principles at least worth considering. When art history or art criticism is our purpose, however, we have found that Marx is misleading. Here other principles prove to have a better claim to priority. In physics and atomic or subatomic analysis of matter, yet other principles prove their merit. And so it goes. I do not say that there are no ways in which these different parts connect: on the contrary, we can only look and see in each case whether there are such conjunctions and of what sort they are.

I used a cube as an image of this view of our understanding and language, but I think there is something to be said for another image, one related to that which Wittgenstein used in speaking of our language as an old city. The image I want to suggest is that of an actual city. Not, I should add, the so-called secular city, but a real city, say any of our great metropolitan cities, such as New York, with its old sections, its odd corners, its multiple villages, its crosscurrents of a financial world and a theatre world and a clothing world and an educational world, and including also its slums and its suburbs. Is it one at all? Well, the answer to that depends on the context in which the question is asked. For some purposes and in certain respects, it is one, in a number of different ways, and no one of these ways tells us all we know or want to know, just as no one jargon will be understood right across the board in every situation of human activity taking place in the city. Some agreement in the use of a common language would appear to be pragmatically necessary for life in any city, but each specific life in the city calls also for some degree of mastery of techniques not common to all. If we gain a clear view of the plurality of language as we use it, we shall have gained important insight into the plurality of our experienced world.

Now how are we to think of a limited God within this pluralistic universe? Suppose there is something in the suggestion that in rejecting the God hypothesis, Bonhoeffer, consciously or unconsciously, more implicitly than explicitly, was reflecting a move into a form of life which operates with the hypothesis of pluralism. Perhaps most of us in the West have also made this move by now. Of what do we speak when we speak of God in this modern metaphysical framework? It seems difficult to draw an analogy from any of the particular powers or forces at work in our actual city. Yet there is one way in which some of us speak sometimes in the city which may provide a clue. Some of us some of the time talk about the spirit of the city. We call it a great little town. Or we talk of it as the wicked city. We say that it is dead, or we say that it has a certain atmosphere of excitement, a life of its own, a character. Sometimes we appeal to this spirit or character in setting out to change something about the city or one small piece of it. Maybe we occasionally find we want to say that we see the heart and spirit of this city embodied in a particular person we have met or know of.

For Bonhoeffer, I suggest, there was such a particular person, "the man-for-others." If you have heard his story, then you have come face-to-face with what gives life to the city, what defines the city, from Bonhoeffer's point of view. This will tell you little or nothing about some of the regulatory problems of the securities exchange. It will not help you at all in determining the best method of mechanical or electronic control of air pollution. It will not tell you whether a given company could survive in the city if it switched a number of its operations to a cybernetic system. The issue of the spirit of the city is important, but it is not omnipotent.

If, however, the question is one of a vision of what life might be in the city, if the question is one of "what it all means," whether it is worthwhile trying to do anything about the mess of the city at all, insofar as this is a question of what I should do now, whether I should accept my own responsibility about the problems of the city, insofar as it is a question of what it means to be a man, in this city, then what I think about the spirit or character of the city, whether I care about the spirit of the city, and concretely, what I find myself using as my image of what it is to be a man in this city may be the most important single thing about me.

The image of man which played this important role for Bonhoeffer was the image he took to be that presented by the New Testament picture of Jesus; but it was important for Bonhoeffer that we approach the New Testament from the Old, that Jesus be seen within the context and against the background of Israel, standing as the center point, as it were, of the image of man expressed in the Old Testament. But did not the men of Israel, and the men of the New Testament, and above all Jesus himself believe in God and speak of God? Of course they did. Yet to ask, "What is God?", (which was the title of the main section of the central chapter of Bonhoeffer's little book, which he never lived to write but which he outlined in one of his last letters), to ask, "What is God?" seems to have been a question which Bonhoeffer found he could answer only indirectly, by speaking of "the man-for-others." It is as if someone were to ask, "But what *is* the spirit of New York?" and the answer were given in the form of telling about the man whom we regarded as the true New Yorker. Insofar as Bonhoeffer was moved to speak of God, a man provided him the terms with which to speak. Within the relative priorities of the city (and the priorities will always be relative in a pluralistic view of how things are), a particular view of a particular man proves to be prior even to a limited God.

When why even speak of a limited God? Is this not really a certain sort of humanism, set within a pluralistic metaphysics? Well, let us say it is at least that. Whatever Bonhoeffer ended as, it was at least as a humanist. But now two things need to be added to qualify this humanism properly, and without these qualifications, it would be misleading to call Bonhoeffer a humanist. First, this particular humanism influences even the model of plurality, leading us to think, for example, of a city rather than of a cube, more adequately developed with the model of a human city than with that of an impersonal cube. It leads us to speak rather anthropomorphically of the city, of its spirit, its character, its pain and suffering, its joys and its life. We would not have caught the force of this humanism if our pluralistic metaphor were mechanistic, so that all we could say about the city would be in terms of its physical characteristics. In thus continuing to grant a privileged status to the language of personhood, Christian theology will always leave its mark on any metaphysical framework in which it operates. This is true of Bonhoeffer's thought, as it is of Karl Barth's.

The second qualification of this particular humanism is that its controlling image of man is of one who spoke in a particular way of a quite particular God. In the Jewish imagination of Jesus and in the Hebrew imagination of his forebears, God was a quite personal figure with a definite character. Those who speak of the spirit of the city and whose imagination is informed by the biblical story will find that they are concerned with the realization of love and justice of the sort that concerned the men of that story, since it was the love and justice which they saw in their God. Imagining God as they did, they lived and spoke as they did and became the men they are presented to have been in that story. The character of that God becomes central in the image of man for those informed by that story.

The conclusion of our investigation may be summarized as follows. The last writings of Bonhoeffer depict a certain form of human life. This is done in human terms, but mixed with them is some of the very oldest language

of Christian theology. Some of that old language, however, was no longer doing its old work. It was acquiring a
new meaning, as a consequence of being used in a new
context and in a new way. Who can say how Bonhoeffer
would have developed in his thinking and language had
he lived? I make no pretense of holding him responsible
for the analysis which I have made. In his last surviving
writings, he was still exploring new uses of old words and
therefore mixing these with some old uses. Understand-
ably the results are often paradoxical. This analysis of one
central paradox suggests that at least one way in which to
move ahead from where Bonhoeffer was will lead us into
a pluralistic metaphysics informed by a christological
humanism, a view of the universe, a way of saying how
things are in our pluralistic city, in which some men may
live lives informed by the biblical story of a man who
lived for others.

That is the hypothesis at which we arrive. Is it a good
hypothesis? Is it useful? Is it true? Well, William James, I
think, was right. The answer to that can only be found
out by the man who dares to gamble on it. Bonhoeffer so
gambled, and I gather he died convinced that he had
won.

N O T E S

[1] My indebtedness for many of the ideas in this paper to the writings
of William James, Stephen Pepper, John Wisdom and Ludwig Wittgenstein will be obvious. Let this general note suffice to indicate this
and to excuse them from any responsibility for the ways in which I
have interpreted their ideas and the use I have made of them.

VII

William James and
Metaphysical Risk

WILLIAM JAMES IS REPORTED BY HIS SISTER TO HAVE SAID of a summer rental: "It's the most delightful house you ever saw; it has fourteen doors, all opening outwards." That house was as if designed for its summer occupant, and for those who want their universe and their ideas complete, neatly arranged and secure, James's philosophy will ever seem too loose and open. It was not intellectual laziness or lack of care that made for this looseness. On the contrary, the character of James's thought and language reflects faithfully the world about which he thought and wrote, the loose, changing, surprising world of our experience, not without order and connections, but not without disorder and disjunction as well. James had a life-long love affair with creation; if he saw this experienced world to be a messy one, he gloried in wearing her scarf of muchness and eachness with a lover's faithfulness. To have accepted the world of the rationalist, the neat closed Universe of the Absolute, to have agreed that "the first morning of creation" wrote "what the last dawn of reckoning shall read,"[1] would have been for James an act of betrayal to the world of radical empiricism.

James was accused by others and by himself of being a popular lecturer, unskilled in and unsympathetic to the careful work of logicians and mathematicians. Although a professor of philosophy for most of his working life, his degree was in medicine, not philosophy, and he began his career at Harvard teaching physiology and anatomy. So described, James hardly sounds worth serious consideration in a volume on the future of American philosophy.

American he certainly was,[2] but was he not a popularizer, a public speaker, a teacher of an era now past? He was all this without question, but I should like in this essay to show from several sides that James was ahead of his critics and warrants a place, not in our history books, but in our contemporary conversation, as one from whom we have something to learn. I intend to do this by discussing five features of James's work: his style, his much criticized case for "the will to believe," his pluralism, his "humanism" and his view of language. In each of these I want to draw out a recurring theme that is important in any further development of a contemporary metaphysics: the place of risk, in the hope of suggesting one possible way through a difficulty that seems to block understanding between English-speaking and Continental philosophy today. I point out that as a theologian, not a philosopher, I see the problems of contemporary philosophy from a certain angle and in connection with particular problems. Whatever limitations this particular approach may have, it is part of what I wish to argue on James's behalf: that its particularity is not only no disqualification, but simply the only way to proceed, frankly accepting one position in the context of many.

It is proper and helpful, I believe, to reflect on the style of James's writing if one wishes to understand his thought. Most of his philosophical work was written to be given as lectures and the style is appropriate to such presentation. At times James expressed regret that this form was inadequate to the intricacies of the subject, but this complaint seems to have expressed his sensitivity to his critics rather than his own view of philosophy. A man's philosophy was the articulation of his style of mind, his form of life, James argued, and this was surely true of James himself. His close friend, Charles Peirce, called his writing "racy" and tried to persuade him that this was no way to write philosophy, a field in which it is proper to employ terms designed to put off the ordinary reader and be available only to those skilled in philosophical argument.[3] The terms, Peirce argued, should be as precise and therefore as far removed from our ordinary discourse as possible. In an interesting anticipation of much later developments in philosophy, James refused his friend's advice, holding for what we have come to call "ordinary language." Rough and ready, popular and down-to-earth as is our ordinary language, there and for that reason is where James wanted to do his work, using just those concrete, robust tools with which in practice we do get about "from next to next" in our ordinary experienced world. The images, examples, and terms of James's arguments were those of a man who wanted above all else to keep his thinking close to "this actual world of finite human lives," and in "the richest intimacy with facts." The ideal of an absolutely precise, logical language was no ideal for one who wanted to speak of this world of flux, the plurality of our experienced world. James took the alternative, and the result is a style marked by charm, even a touch of elegance, no small wit and a robustness that calls the reader to share James's far from uncritical love affair with the whole of our experienced world.[4] No naïve cultural or naturalistic optimism followed from this, for James. Leibniz's *Théodicée*, defending this world and all its evils as the best of all possible worlds led James to remark that the author's "feeble grasp of reality is too obvious to need comment from me. It is evident that no realistic image of the experience of a "damned" soul had ever approached the portals of his mind."[5]

To resort to "ordinary language" is to run a risk which can be expressed by saying that our philosophy will be no more airtight, no more logical, than our lives. "Precisely," thought William James, and smiled. That was exactly where he wanted to be and the style in which he wanted to do his philosophizing. The advantages of accepting this risk were more subtly expressed later in the way in which Wittgenstein worked his way free of the *Tractatus*, but I think that even Wittgenstein did not learn as well as James how to smile on this "rough ground" without absolutes. The charm of James's style is the mark of the success with which he was able to free himself from any vestigial longing for a world secured by an absolute or a guarantee of truth or perfection.

Time and again over the years, James apologized for having chosen the title "The Will to Believe" for an early essay. What he meant, and said clearly enough in the essay itself, was that we have a *right* to believe, that there is a justification for beliefs in certain sorts of matters, although we have only partial evidence for any definite conclusion. There are cases, James argued, when we must choose one belief or another, and in such cases not to choose is only to make another choice. Critics of this essay and its central thesis, from its appearance through Bertrand Russell, have justified James's frequent complaint that they objected to the title, apparently without having read the essay itself. James did not claim that our beliefs about the world were simply a matter of will. "Just try and see if you can make yourself believe that Abraham Lincoln never existed," was James's response in anticipation of that absurd idea. Nor did he recommend jumping to conclusions where further evidence was available for the looking. But James did mean that our jump to a conclusion in some important matters was itself a piece of the picture we wanted to understand, itself part of the state of affairs about which a conclusion had to be made. In such questions as whether life is worth living, whether novelty is possible in this world, whether we have free will, and whether our actions add something to the makeup of the future, we must decide without knowing "for sure," and the way in which we choose will itself contribute to the making of a world in which our belief works and thus proves itself to be true. These jumps create in part the conditions of their own realization, making for the truth of the position which we chose.[6]

The aspect of this thesis to which I wish to draw attention is the nature of one sort of question to which James felt it applied. In the essay in which he first propounded the thesis, James focused on two sorts of questions, the moral and the religious, or, lest we construe these more narrowly than James, the questions, "What do you think of yourself? What do you think of the world?" Neither logical demonstration nor empirical verification will be able to settle these questions. How we take things to be, the frame of reference within which we establish what we are going to take into account in any proof, is not itself capable of proof in the same ways.

Long before the issue was posed in the thirties, James was aware that we deal with many more sorts of problems than those which can be settled by logical demonstration or empirical verification. He urged the use of empirical verification wherever it was applicable and thought we should always try to ask the pragmatic question, demanding what he called the "cash value" of a proposition.[7] But James realized that we are concerned for other matters, that we have questions which such procedures will not settle, and among these are questions of religion and metaphysics. These questions, which he frequently posed as questions about how we are to use words (the question concerning the good or truth he usually dealt with as a question of how we use the words "good" and "true") are those which have to do with the way in which we see the world and our place in it.

During the course of his life, James came to view the serious work of philosophy more and more as the study of metaphysics, and as James applied himself to this study, his way of working bears interesting anticipations of the "revolution in philosophy" of a generation later.[8] He would have been comfortable with a later understanding of metaphysics as a clarification of the ways in which we say how things are, as one or another proposal to see in a particular way what we have been looking at all along. The question about facts, for James, had to do with how we are to use the word "fact," and his conclusion was that a "fact" was what we carved the world up into, our way of coming to terms with our experienced world, ever in part a product of our own view of things.

To carve out facts in some particular way, to detect patterns in the world, to see the world in a certain way, was a matter of belief, a venture involving risk. As James saw it, there was no getting around this. Metaphysics meant one choice or another, one belief or another, and, therefore, risk—no matter which way one moved. He saw this and he did not recoil. He took life and this world to be really open-ended, dangerous, and venturesome, and he liked it that way. "I am willing that there should be real losses and real losers. . . . When the cup is poured off, the dregs are left behind for ever, but the possibility of what is poured off is sweet enough to accept."[9] What distinguishes the thought of James from so many philosophers before and since his time is not so much that he saw the element of risk in all human thought and action, but that he felt that this gave life a high flavor.

Nowhere does this character of James's thought become more evident than in his championing of one side of what he repeatedly called "the most pregnant issue in metaphysics," the issue of the one and the many and his devotion to the choice of pluralism. The title of his Hibbert Lectures, *A Pluralistc Universe*, but more especially the way in which he introduced the subject in his Lowell Lectures, leads us to what James meant by pluralism. The world is one, James argued, in some important ways. It is one as a "universe of discourse," one by our way of speaking of it as a universe, a totality. Then it is one insofar as we can pass from here to there and from then to now by means of the continuities of space and time. The universe is also one as it is connected by lines of influence and by causal connections which we detect; it is one insofar as we create lines of connection by our human efforts. The world is one, that is, in more ways than one. The form of the presentation has already made the point: the "universe" is not one thing but a number of things, a number of ways of slicing up what experience runs into, and in each case, it is one "in so far forth." " 'The world is One,' therefore, just so far as we experience it to be concatenated, One by as many definite conjunctions as appear. But then also *not* One by just as many definite disjunctions as we find. The oneness and the manyness of it thus obtain in respects which can be separately named. It is neither a universe pure and simple nor a multiverse pure and simple."[10]

The form and style of the argument is an important

part of what James was driving at. The metaphysics of pluralism must itself be open to the plurality of experience, the plurality, we would say today, of language games. Each of these may have its own justification in its own usefulness for our getting along with some aspect of our experienced world. Insofar as each language game can actually be played, insofar is it to be allowed its place. But there are other games to play as well, and the pluralist asks only that we allow that thus far we have not learned how to do justice to each by subsuming them all under one set of rules.

Resting as it does on what we find to obtain, it is evident that such a metaphysics cannot be dogmatic. An absolute pluralism would be a contradiction in terms. It would close off the future, excluding in advance the possibility of greater or higher degrees of unity yet to be detected or constructed. That would be, not James's pluralism, but atomism. In doing battle with any and every sort of monism with the weapon of "ever not quite," James never defended an atomism of any sort. It was in this connection that he criticized the empiricism of Locke and Hume, which he distinquished from his own radical empiricism. By "radical empiricism" James meant that we must take seriously and start always from a position open to all of our experience. We do not experience the world as so many discrete sense-data, so many distinct billiard balls. On the contrary, we experience the world as a world, albeit a world in more ways than one, with no one way serving all purposes. Causal, aesthetic, political, economic and linguistic connections are as much a part of the "what" of our experience as any "this" or "that." Logically, perhaps, atomism is the opposite of monism, but for a radical empiricist, the alternative fashioned by "ever not quite" had to be pluralism.

"Ever not quite" was not only a weapon with which James fought Royce and the rest of his philosophic foes; it was also the standard for his own metaphysical camp. The metaphysics of pluralism as James presented it is— one might almost say in principle (a precursor of Gödel's theorem)—unfinished, subject to genuine novelty. The editor of *Some Problems of Philosophy*, on which James was working when he died, not misleadingly used the word "Novelty" in each of the chapter headings for the last third of this work. Novelty, risk, reorganization are built into this view of things by the same factors which exclude any monistic metaphysics. The world may yet be one, James insisted, only we don't see how this can be, and a great deal counts against this being the case at present. It may yet be one, in the sense not only that it may be one in some way which our experience of it does not let us see, but it may be one in the sense that its unity may lie ahead of us. The universe may be growing into one, in some sense not clear to us. James's metaphysics and all his philosophical work was future-oriented. The theoretical possibility of unity in things was, he felt, a question about the future, and one of his repeated objections to rationalists was that they pointed to a unity already established. James's universe was unfinished, open to the future. It was a world-in-the-making.

This open-ended, future-oriented, unfinished character of the universe of pluralism was connected with James's belief in free will, the conviction that men can and do change the world, actually change it, so that the genuinely new comes into play by human choice.[11] The world-being-made is being made by us, to some extent. The issue here, James insisted, was not theoretical but practical. The issue was pragmatic, for if belief were not a philosophical belief for living, what interest could it have? The question that matters in life is what we shall make of life, what is to happen to our world. James was, we may say, existentially interested in this question, or, in his terms, pragmatically interested. A metaphysical view of things or a view of the universe as unfinished, still in the making, with ourselves as responsible in some ascertainable ways for what is to become of our world, a metaphysics involving risk, is the consequence of the method of pragmatism built on radical empiricism.[12]

Perhaps at this point we can begin to see one way in which two apparently divergent lines of thought in James's idea of God may be seen to be consistent. On the one hand, James argued that God should be conceived as an ultimate, not an absolute. The Absolute, for James, was the great first principle of the rationalist mind which stood at the center of a monistic universe, prior to everything else in every sense of the word. The Absolute held all things together and all things were of and from the absolute. Against this idea James set the ultimate, the telos that may yet appear, the unity of things that may yet arise. The absolute is from eternity; the ultimate has to be realized, and that means that the ultimate has to be realized in part by us if it is ever to be. God is the end toward which we press, the goal for which we strive, not the creator from which all comes. All this sounds close to Dewey's definition of God as the sum of our ideals, the unification of our ideal ends.

There is, however, another way in which James speaks of God.[13] God is, in other places, a limited, active agent in things, one element within the many forces at work in the universe. God is but one entity within the plurality of this universe, not certain to win and not assuredly the most powerful entity, needing our help as much as we need his in order that a better world may have a chance of being realized. In connection with this line of thought, James suggested that the appropriate religion for a pluralist would be polytheism, but he seemed to have felt that, as polytheism was transformed into monotheism, the religious (as distinct from the philosophical) interest in God had retained the original polytheistic sense of the divine: God as but one helper among many.

If we keep in the foreground the element of risk in James's metaphysics, these two strains in his thought may be seen to be less incompatible than they appear when simply set side by side. As a radical empiricist, and on the basis of his studies of religious experience, James seems to have felt that he could not discount the possibility of some higher or other consciousness than that of ordinary men. He had no religious experiences of his own to go on, but even in the later part of his life, in the writings coming from the time after he had finished his Gifford Lectures and had turned his attention centrally to the problems of metaphysics, James seemed to remain open to God as a possible hypothesis. The God that seemed to James possible, however, was a limited God in a pluralistic universe, concerned for men as religion said he was, but surely not omnipotent.[14] Whether or not this God (this idea of God) would turn out to be ultimate, whether he would be the telos of our life and world, was, for James, an open question. There was a risk in this enterprise for God as for man, and the outcome was in important respects in our hands. If we hold these elements in James's thought together, we see that he was not saying the same thing as Dewey, for Dewey seemed to be sure that God was but the name for our human ideals. For James, God was at least this, but perhaps this was not the last word. Here too the open-ended character of his metaphysics is evident. The metaphysical story, if it is truly a story about the universe of our human experience is a story not yet finished. In this way, James, although not what one would call a religious man himself, sought to justify religion, in the sense that he tried to leave a door open for its claim. To a religion that claimed to have the secret of all questions, however, that promised final, inevitable and perfect victory, as to the atheist who cried that all religion was absurd, James would answer quietly, "ever not quite." Pluralism meant for James a profound willingness to reside without regret in an unfinished universe, a world still in the making, avowing the risk involved in human existence and the existence of our world.

Metaphysical risk can be expressed by saying, simply, human metaphysics. Metaphysics as an account of how things are is always a human account, a view of things which is our view. However chastening this thought may be to the metaphysician, it was one of which James never lost sight. In all our ideas, concepts, understandings and truths, "you can't weed out the human contribution." James seems to have held by this before he ever borrowed Schiller's name of "humanism" for it. He was trained and began teaching as a natural scientist, but he was no believer in scientism or in any form of scientific naturalism. He was a verificationist, but one who knew that any verification held only in the terms that we set up for the process of verification.[15] The result was that James was constantly concerned for truths, not Truth, and ever argued that "Truth" is a pursuit as changing and living and growing as the ones who pursue it.

Although every truth is someone's truth, all thought and language being in this sense relative to the thinker and speaker, still there are strong checks against solipsism and against the total devaluation and leveling of all ideas which such a relativistic theory might at first suggest. As we saw that opposition to monism led James by no means to atomism, that being for him only a theoretical not a practical alternative, so in this case opposition to the rationalist belief in Truth did not lead to the total relativity of all ideas. James argued that "truth" is a word we use for our ideas, for what we *say* about our experienced world. Our experienced world is not true or false, it just is; but when we come to speak of it, to hold certain ideas about it, then the question of truth is important. Not any idea goes. Some ideas are more true, some are false. The issue is settled, again pluralistically, in more than one way. An idea is true if it leads me on from next to next in my experience, if I find that with it I can make useful and helpful connections in my experienced world. There is a further control on our ideas, however, which James called "common sense," the "funded truths" of our own past experience and the experience of those who have gone before us. A new idea has to fit in with the old ideas somehow. There may have to be changes, corrections, of the new idea or of some of the old ones, before this fitting in can take place, but if the idea is to be true for me, it has to come to terms with all the other truths, all the other beliefs which I have. That rules out capriciousness. A new scientific theory, for example, in order to work, "must derange common sense and previous belief as little as possible, and it must lead to some sensible terminus or other that can be verified exactly. To 'work' means both these things; and the squeeze is so tight that there is little loose play for any hypothesis."[16] The "squeeze" from the side of "common sense," however, means that the question of any truth is a human, social enterprise. Some "Truth" which was not someone's truth was no truth for James.

This view of the human risk in all thought enabled James to see the human element in everything we say about the world. The picture of pure facts "out there" as over against our possibly distorted view of them "in here" was precisely what James objected to in the rationalist metaphysics of his day. It is important to see that James did not have to fight against this in his own mind; he was not in the least tempted by such a view of reality. "The notion of a reality calling us to 'agree' with it, and that for no reasons, but simply because its claim is 'unconditional' or 'transcendent,' is one that I can make neither head nor tail of. I try to imagine myself as the sole reality of the world. . . . What good it would do me to be copied [by a human mind], or what good it would do that mind to copy me, if further consequences are expressly and in principle ruled out as motives for the claim (as they are by our rationalist authorities) I cannot fathom. When the Irishman's admirers ran him along to the place of banquet in a sedan chair with no bottom, he said, 'Faith, if it wasn't for the honor of the thing, I might as well have come on foot.' "[17]

In an important and unavoidable way, facts are man-made. We carve out groups of stars and call them constellations, "and the stars suffer us patiently to do so," our scientific theories are our human reports of nature, and facts are what we carve our world up into. But if facts are what we carve the world up into, it is terribly important to us that we do this, and that we do it in some ways and not in others. In no way did James mean to denigrate facts or theories or constellations. In no sense did he think it made no difference how we carved up our experienced world. But he did insist that however we went about this, the human element was always part of it and that our metaphysics ought to be honest about this.

James put his point graphically by saying, "we are not the readers but the very personages of the world-drama." Some supposed world of pure facts, or of things-in-themselves, or of absolute Truth untouched by the human element, any way of speaking of reality as though it lay "back there" somewhere beyond, behind, or other than the world of our experience, was for James nonsensical and even repellent and he used all his skill to try to wean us away from such a view of things.

The last and, for our present situation, the most important aspect of James's thought has to do with the risk involved in language. Wittgenstein once formulated the gnawing question which can lead us astray in this matter in these words: "Is there some reality lying behind the notation which shapes its grammar?"[18] Wittgenstein's whole aim was *not* to answer "No," but to lead us away from trying to answer this question at all, from so construing philosophy that we allow the slim edge of the old philosophical wedge to slip in between "reality" and our language. In contrast to those who would say that there is a reality behind our language to which it points or which it reflects, and also to those who would say there is no such reality, or not one we can know, he wanted us to learn to look at language in such a way that this question would not even arise. The only world I can talk about is the world I can talk about, Wittgenstein seems desperately to have wanted to say, and that he wanted to say this desperately is perhaps the problem. James did not seem to be desperate but took this important tautology as his starting point in its basic form: the world we experience (speak of) is the world we experience (speak of). Our talk about the world may prove with further experience and talking to need emendation. That risk, the fact that we have to do our talking and understanding, as it were, from within our words and our understanding, the self-referential character of all speaking and thinking, was what Wittgenstein saw, and his later philosophy was a struggle to get over feeling that this was an unfortunate limitation to our language. James, on the other hand, saw this and seemed to have no feeling that it might have been otherwise. He was, if I may put it that way, comfortable with the element of risk, of insecurity, that characterizes all language and thought. Wittgenstein was haunted by the ghost of an older philosophy that whispered about a reality (of course, ineffable, of course, beyond my experience, yet surely the foundation of my experience, for if I experience something, there must be that something which I experience) which hovered behind our words, with which our words ought to correspond. He tried to lay that ghost, to still forever the suggestion of a real behind our talk about the real. How easily we are seduced by our language itself into listening to this whisper! I think it can be said that James was not haunted by this ghost, however more simple the problem seemed to him. Had Wittgenstein met James, I believe he would have gone away muttering to himself, "It's all so much more complex than he is aware of, so much more subtle." But he would also have gone away filled with envy! He would surely have been right about the problem being more complex than the way in which James saw it, but that James saw it in such a way that it really was not a problem for him, that he knew the risk in metaphysics and was at peace, that he was aware of the self-referential character of all language and did not want or try to evade it, is a feature of his thought that commends him to our attention in the present situation in philosophy.

The point which I am making may be clearer if we see it more directly in James's work. Wittgenstein detected more than one problem in James, due to his not having consistently seen the linguistic form of philosophical problems.[19] That Wittgenstein made a remarkable advance over James in this matter cannot be denied. But James was quite consciously interested in the problem of language, and this is evident enough from any of his later works. His pragmatism was a rough anticipation of the use theory of words: find the cash value of a word, see how the word is used, its "particular go," and many a problem can be dissolved, James argued. This approach is evident even in some of his earlier essays. The words chance and gift, for example, he saw as two importantly different sides of the same coin, "the one begin simply a disparaging, and the other a eulogistic, name for anything on which we have no effective claim."[20] Language is how we come to terms with the world, for without "adjectives and adverbs and predicates and heads of classification and conceptions" we would not be able to handle "the real world" at all.[21] Language is a rough tool, perhaps, and nothing we say in words is ever all that is to be said; something is always left over. But this was not for James an invitation to chase the will-o'-the-wisp of some reality beyond our words, some supposed real world abstracted from or posited behind our experienced world.

In an important essay with a typically Jamesian title, "The Sentiment of Rationality," James said: "In every proposition whose bearing is universal (and such are all the propositions of philosophy), the acts of the subject and their consequences throughout eternity should be included in the formula. If M represent the entire world *minus* the reaction of the thinker upon it, and if $M+x$ represent the absolutely total matter of philosophic propositions (x standing for the thinker's reaction and its results), what would be a universal truth if the term x were of one complexion, might become egregious error if x altered its character."[22] All propositions of philosophy, and not least those of metaphysics, are of the $M+x$ sort. The question about the world is always the question of what we say about the world, how we are to speak, and it is solely of our speaking that the question of truth is in order. To ask if our speaking of the world is true is to ask not about the past, however, not about some conformity of our words with an eternally settled "that," but about the future, about how we can move ahead with these words. "Fact," as we have mentioned, is for James our word for moving ahead with our experienced world. James no more than Wittgenstein doubted that there was an experienced world which we run up against with our word "fact," and woe to us if we misuse the word. The word whose leading we cannot follow, the use of a word which blocks our movement from next to next may exact a high price.

What Wittgenstein was trying to make clear was already clear to William James. It was clear in his radical empiricism, which freed him to see that the only world we can talk of is the world we do talk of, and it was clear in his pragmatism, which rested its case and tested every other case by asking that we follow the leading of our language and see where it took us. James in his own way had said, "Don't think, but look!"

If the metaphysician stands unavoidably within the picture he is trying to get clear about, if he is an actor, a *dramatis persona* in the drama of the universe, his description of that universe, his proposal for how it shall be seen and spoken of is itself a part of that universe and his proposal or description must be taken into account as one factor in deciding whether that description will turn out to have been helpful, "true" in James's sense of the word. Life and language are one, for James as for Wittgenstein, and to speak of life is to take a step into life's future, following the leading of our language.

How can we know that the leading will prove satisfactory? Much can be brought to bear on this which can help us from mistakes, but, in the last analysis, we cannot know for sure in advance. Here we must decide, for to wait until all the evidence is in is to wait for evidence that will include the fact that we sat and waited. Therefore the safest course, paradoxically, is to take the risk. I have found only one reference that indicates directly that James may have read Kierkegaard ("We must live forwards, a Danish thinker has said, but we understand backwards."[23]), but their agreement in this important area is clear. To live is risk, to speak is risk, and to seek some other security at this point is to turn one's back on life. If we are to use language (and how else shall we be human?), then we must use our human language with its self-referential character.[24] No appeal to a pure logic, to any supposed a priori that is prior to our mastery of the technique which is language, no assertion of an absolute Truth or any other M without an x can change this character of the language we use.

The objections to this were not wanting. " 'In other words,' an opponent might say, 'resolve your intellect into a kind of slush.' 'Even so,' I make reply,—'if you will consent to use no politer word.' For humanism, conceiving the more 'true' as the more 'satisfactory' (Dewey's term), has sincerely to renounce rectilinear arguments and ancient ideals of rigor and finality. It is in just this temper of renunciation, so different from that of pyrrhonistic scepticism, that the spirit of humanism essentially consists. Satisfactoriness has to be measured by a multitude of standards, of which some, for aught we know, may fail in any given case; and what is more satisfactory than any alternative in sight, may to the end be a sum of *pluses* and *minuses,* concerning which we can only trust that by ulterior corrections and improvements a maximum of the one and a minimum of the other may someday be approached. It means a real change of heart, a break with absolutistic hopes, when one takes up this inductive view of the conditions of belief."[25]

James has been mostly known by students of theology and religion through his *Varieties of Religious Experience.* This is too bad. That book marks a turning point in James's work, the last fruits of the experimental psychologist, only in the last chapter pointing to what had already become his chief interest and was to occupy the rest of his years, a subject far more important for the present problems of religious thought: metaphysics. James could have lived happily with a later conception of metaphysics already mentioned: a proposal to view things in a particular way. James would have wanted to underscore that it is always our view, *our* way of saying how things are, that is at stake, and that how we come out on this matter is as important for our life and our world as anything else about us. A crucial feature of James's metaphysics, I have tried to show, is the avowal of risk, and it is at this point that James has something to say to our present religio-philosophical situation. Theology today is bogged down in gross misunderstandings between those who look to certain "existentialist" philosophers, sure that the rest of us have turned our back on the real issue of language's involvement in life, and those who walk with analytic philosophy and find certain French or German thinkers hopelessly entangled in category blunders. Perhaps James could help both sides, and American religious thought could do worse than follow some of the leads provided by William James in seeing that to accept metaphysical risk and to acknowledge the self-referential character of language, being two sides of the same coin, have the same "cash value."

NOTES

1. *Some Problems of Philosophy* (New York, 1911), p. 189.
2. That is not a parochial judgment: *"Il a pu passer en Amérique pour le plus cosmoplite et en Europe pour le plus américain des philosophes."* M. Le Breton, *La Personalité de William James,* 1925, p. 35.
3. Review of James's *Principles of Psychology, The Nation,* Peirce's *Collected Papers,* Vol. 8, p. 57.
4. *Cf.* James's correspondence, especially with his brother, and commentary in Perry, *The Thought and Character of William James,* 1935, Vol. 1, *passim. Cf.* also Warner Berthoff's discussion of James's style in his *The Ferment of Realism; American Literature 1884-1919* (New York: Free Press, 1965).
5. *Pragmatism,* p. 30. *Cf.* the discussion following, pp. 30-33.
6. *The Will to Believe. Cf. The Sentiment of Rationality;* also lecture 8 of *A Pluralistic Universe,* New York, 1909, pp. 317f.
7. *Pragmatism.* The second lecture is as clear a presentation of this as can be found in James's writings.
8. James's growing interest in philosophy and especially in metaphysics is evident in his published work and well presented in Perry, *op. cit.* Some examples of his use of the "verification principle," his recognition of its limits, its metaphysical character, and also of his analysis of language, can be found in his *Pragmatism,* especially the second, sixth and seventh lectures.
9. *Pragmatism,* pp. 190f.; *Cf.* pp. 187f; *Some Problems of Philosophy,* Chap. IXff.

10. *Pragmatism*, pp. 100f.

11. "Free-will pragmatically means *novelties in the world,* the right to expect that in its deepest elements as well as in its surface phenomena, the future may not identically repeat and imitate the past." *Pragmatism*, p. 84.

12. *Ibid.,* p. 187f.

13. This second way of speaking of God, as a higher consciousness, but limited, characterizes the conclusion of his Gifford Lectures. It needs to be balanced by his treatment of religious belief and God in his later Lowell and Hibbert Lectures, as well as in some of his other essays. A letter to Thomas Davison quoted by Perry, *op. cit.,* Vol. I, pp. 737f., is to be noted. Of the early essays, "Reflex Action and Theism" is especially worth attention.

14. "When John Mill said that the notion of God's omnipotence must be given up, if God is to be kept as a religious object, he was surely accurately right; yet so prevalent is the lazy monism that idly haunts the region of God's name, that so simple and truthful a saying was generally treated as a paradox: God, it was said, *could* not be finite. I believe that the only God worthy of the name *must* be finite." *A Pluralistic Universe*, pp. 124-125.

15. *Cf.* "The Sentiment of Rationality," *Essays on Faith and Morals* (Cleveland: World Publishing Co., 1962), especially p. 94 and note.

16. *Pragmatism*, p. 142.

17. *Ibid.,* p. 152.

18. *Philosophical Investigations,* §562.

19. *Ibid,* §342. *Cf.* §§610, 342, and in Part II, p. 219.

20. "The Dilemma of Determinism," *Essays on Faith and Morals*, p. 159.

21. *Varieties* (New York, 1902), p. 56. That James would not be totally lost in contemporary analytic discussion may be indicated by the following, from *Some Problems of Philosophy*, pp. 199f.: "The conceptualist rule is to suppose that where there is a separate name there ought to be a fact as separate; and Hume, following this rule, and finding no such fact corresponding to the word 'power,' concludes that the word is meaningless. By this rule every conjunction and preposition in human speech is meaningless—*in, on, of, with, but, and, if* are as meaningless as *for,* and *because.* The truth is that neither the elements of fact nor the meanings of our words are separable as the words are. The original form in which fact comes is the perceptual *durcheinander*, holding terms as well as relations in solution, or interfused and cemented. Our reflective mind abstracts diverse aspects in the muchness, as a man looking through a tube may limit his attention to one part

after another of a landscape. But abstraction is not insulation; and it no more breaks reality than the tube breaks the landscape. Concepts are notes, views taken on reality, not pieces of it, as bricks are part of a house."

22. "Sentiment of Rationality," *op. cit.*, pp. 97f.

23. *Pragmatism*, p. 146. The fact that just this same remark occurs in *A Pluralistic Universe*, p. 244, suggests that this may have been picked up somewhere and was all of S. K. that James knew.

24. On the inevitably self-referential character of all distinctively human language, *cf.* Jacob Bronowski, "The Logic of Mind," *American Scientist*, Vol. 54, No. 1, 1966.

25. "Humanism and Truth," from *The Meaning of Truth*, in *Pragmatism*, p. 232.

VIII

Is Transcendence
the Word We Want?

IN A RECENT ARTICLE SUBTITLED "TRANSCENDENCE WITH-out mythology,"[1] Professor Gordon Kaufman has attempted "to show that the meaning of the word 'God,' even in its reference to the 'transcendent,' can be developed and understood entirely in terms of this-worldly (i.e., 'secular') experiences and conceptions—that is, in terms fully comprehensible and significant to the most 'modern' of men—and that therefore the whole issue of a presupposed cosmological dualism, so problematic for modern man, can be by-passed."[2] I could have chosen as well any number of similar statements from many other "younger" theologians, my own included, but this statement will serve nicely as a definition of the intention or purpose of much of the work of the so-called new theology. Although I shall have a word to say about Kaufman's proposal for how we should proceed, I want to begin by asking some questions about this task in which so many of us now seem to be engaged.

The most painful and least considered question that can be asked about this task which we have set for ourselves is simply, "Why?" There is something slightly fantastic in this attempt to understand God in terms of human experience, and if we find we are unable or unwilling to face up to the inner motives which lead us to embark on this strange quest, we should at least admit that the quest is a rather odd one. I should judge that few men have spoken seriously of God, or, with a correction from Buber worth pondering, few men have dared or cared to speak to God. Or, if we judge that all words are foolish and inappropriate on such occasions, then let us say that few are they who have trembled in a situation which they might later describe as being "in the presence of" the gods, or God. With whatever words we choose to speak of such an occasion, is it seriously our concern to make *this* experience, whether our's or that of another, understandable in the terms provided by the rest of our experience? Would this not be as difficult an undertaking as trying to translate the language of love into the language of biology? I admit that this can be done, but I do not think it unreasonable to admit that something is lost in the process. Why this urge, then, to make one language game normative for another and rather different language game? Or more to the point, what sort of language game is this in which one tries to translate "God" into the language of "this-worldly (i.e., 'secular') experiences and conceptions?"

It seems to be everyone's right to define "modern man" for himself these days, and all of us in the "new theology" have done it in our own ways. When we have done so, however, few of us seem to have had in mind the man who trembles, be it but once in his life, "in the presence of the Gods." Is it because we have not so trembled ourselves that we wish to make that man's peculiar gift—or curse—available to us on our own terms? Why can't we leave that strange soul alone, let him be himself, not ask of him that he make his fearful experience a marketable commodity, available to every "modern man"? Is not the genius of religion that it is not every man's dish of tea, not a marketable commodity, not something to be had on whatever terms any of us might be willing to pay? I think these questions are fair, although I am not sure that I have the courage to stand up to them.

The next question is but a little less painful. Why do we try to translate the word "God" at all? If as Kaufman argues (correctly in my judgment), this word is bound up in its traditional use with "the fundamental meta-physical-cosmological dualism found in the Bible (as well as in traditional metaphysics) and in virtually all Western religious thought,"[3] why try to extract it from that context? We do not try to do this with the gods of the Greek dramatists. If we visit Olympia and wander through its groves, or climb slowly and meditatively the Via Sacra of Delphi, are we not willing to let the gods of Greece be themselves? Do we understand the Greeks better by demythologizing their understandings of things? Of course, we are Christians, we say, whatever we mean by that, so the weight of the long history of Christianity hangs over us as a great burden which we try to justify to ourselves as "modern men." We are free enough to let the Greeks be the Greeks. We are not free to let the Hebrews be the Hebrews, but must show that everything from urbanization in the twentieth century to constitutional democratic politics, as we now play it, is all rooted deep in the strange writings come down to us from that ancient Semite tribal system of long ago. Even the Church Fathers of the fifth century have no peace from us but must

be pushed and shoved around to fit into our current conversation as though they too had been products of our
times, not of their own. Is nothing sacred to us "new
theologians?"

"Men of other ages," Kaufman says, "found it necessary
to create and believe elaborate mythologies and metaphysics of the 'beyond' in order to understand their world
and themselves. Contemporay men in contrast . . . find it
more and more unnecessary and even ridiculous to make
this dualistic assumption."[4] Yes, but now two things must
be said. There are contemporary men and contemporary
men. If I am right that there have been few in any age
who have "trembled in the presence of the gods," then
what either ancient or contemporary man found or finds
possible or agreeable is beside the point. If those in ages
past who trembled before the gods found their own
peculiar way of speaking and living, the question could
well be, whether we are interested in making such a distinction in our day. Are we all of a piece, all modern men,
or are there among us today the many and the few, the
many who make up the largest part of all establishments,
religious or otherwise, and the few, the strange ones, who
tremble and stand in awe, however they may choose to
speak of it?

Second, if we grant that only some men could have
ever been said to have "trembled in the presence of the
gods," must we assume this same thing goes on today?
Perhaps, in some sense, we may. That is to say, perhaps
we could say that there is a sense of things, a kind of
experience, which men in the past might have called

"being in the presence of the gods." Perhaps, on the basis of some sort of analysis, it could be argued that the same sort of sense or experience is occasionally to be found today. No doubt today, men who know of this sort of thing first-hand have their own ways of speaking of such matters if they speak of it at all. If such men say that their experience is the same, that is, if they find that the way men spoke in the past speaks still to them of what has happened to them, I would judge they have some grounds for saying that it was "the same thing." I am not sure that they would really care terribly whether the rest of us decided it was the same or different. I should think that for these few for whom these matters are first-hand, the question of whether their experience and that of Socrates and Isaiah were the same would be secondary. The rest of us should worry less about similarities and dissimilarities until we have a clearer understanding among us about what today, in our own terms and for ourselves, we wish to be talking about. When that is at least clearer than it now seems to be, we may find it matters less than we thought whether we use the old language and speak of being "in the presence of the Gods" or find other words. If Gordon Kaufman is right that we are really interested in talking about human experience, maybe we can learn to relax a bit over the issue of some ancient ways of speaking.

These questions about the present undertaking of us "new theologians" brings me to what I take to be a central problem in the "new theology." If we are seriously interested in the experience of the few, as distinct from the experiences of the many, what is it about the experience of the strange ones, what is it about their language that interests us? Gordon Kaufman proposes that we should focus on "man's sense of limitation, finitude, guilt, and sin, on the one hand, and his question about the meaning or value or significance of himself, his life, and his world, on the other," for here is where language about God emerges or has emerged.[5] I have two objections to raise at this point. The first is that whatever experience we have in mind when we think of men speaking of the gods, it has surely been the experience of the strange ones in any society. Surely there have been men in different eras who have had a deep sense of limitation and agonizing questions about the meaning of life. Even if we judge this a very Augustinian view of the matter, still, the influence of Augustine has been tremendous in the West. But Augustine was a strange one himself, and his *Confessions* remain his own, not a document of the common self-understanding of late fourth century Roman civilization. It is not "man's sense of limitation," but certain men's sense of limitation which gives rise to language about God.

My more basic objection, however, is that a sense of limitation is too narrow a definition of the experiential rootage of the language about the gods even for Christianity. There is more to Christianity than Augustine. To put it in a way more in line with my opening questions, the strange ones of our age are too narrowly delineated by this sense of limitation. I am certainly willing to grant that some of the strange ones of this world have wrestled with a sense of limitation and out of this struggle have been led to speak of the gods. I surely do not wish to make Augustine the villain of the story; but he is not the whole story. Indeed, I do not see why this Augustinian motif must be taken as normative for exploring the ways in which men have spoken of the gods in the past, or for distinguishing the strange ones from the masses in any era. I propose, in order to widen the field, indeed in order to provide a rather different approach to our common task in theology today, that we could better define our focus.

Without excluding Gordon Kaufman's proposal, I suggest that we use a sense of wonder, rather than limitation, as the point of departure. Speech about God, or silence about God, for that matter, but in any case, the sort of speech and the sort of silence that marks off the strange ones from the masses, the deep ones from the superficial, appears within the context of a sense of wonder, awe, and joy before what is there for all to behold; the fact that we are alive, that there is anything at all. The mystical, as Wittgenstein put it, and he was surely one of the strange ones, is not how the world is, but *that* it is.[6] This sense of awe and wonder occurs when one is *struck* by the fact that I am, and that I am I, that a tree is itself, that there is anything at all, in short when all these things, oddly enough, no longer seem to be self-evident to us and no cause for surprise. It is wonder at and joy in the concreteness and specificness of things, more than in their limitedness. (If the traditionally minded are here inclined to say that I am arguing the priority of creation to sin, I can only say that if that is what I had wanted to say I would have said it.)

If we proceed from this starting point to understand what can also be called the religious aspect of man, we will not start, as Gordon Kaufman has, with an analysis of man's finitude, leading to an idea of God as a limiting concept, but rather we begin with the concreteness and specificness of our life, its possibilities and its problems, and if the word "God" appears—or if it does not—the decisive point to be made is that some men are *struck* by the ordinary, whereas most find it only ordinary.

Kaufman recognizes that we cannot, apparently, escape some sort of duality, no matter how "secular" we are. The duality he proposes is that of "experience and its Limit(s)." I propose as an alternative the duality of the ordinary seen as ordinary and the ordinary seen as extraordinary. About this proposal I wish to say something in response to Kaufman's concern to make clear "the actual base *in concrete experience* from which theological work proceeds" in order to give "an interpretation of religious language which could justify its use to contemporary secular man."[7] Whoever "contemporary secular man" is supposed to be, I should think he would assume that religious language is rooted in concrete experience. Perhaps some oversimplified Freudian view of the matter would hold for a good many "contemporary secular men." If he has doubts about the matter, what he doubts is the validity of proceeding to theology from these experiences, not that there are experiences from which to proceed. But why in the world should we be interested in trying to justify religious language to this hypothetical man? How, for that matter, is he going to justify *his* language to the religious man? Isn't the issue between them precisely over what constitutes a justification? Let me put it in terms of the duality which I have proposed. A sees a situation as extraordinary and a cause for wonder, so that, given certain assumptions about his past and the person to whom he is speaking afterwards, he might say that he had been "in the presence of the gods" (although this particular way of talking is but one of many that might be used, and today a rather unlikely one). B sees exactly the same situation as ordinary and says so. Now what shall we say of this? Was it exactly the same situation that both saw? Is it not yet a third way to see the situation, when we are aware that two men have seen the situation differently? It seems to be the case that there is no alternative to seeing things *as*. Every seeing is "seeing as." Depending on our purposes, what we wish to accomplish, the context, and many other factors, we shall have what we call grounds for seeing a situation in one way rather than in another. But seeing the "ordinary" as extraordinary, as a cause for wonder, is no more and no less in need of justification than seeing the "ordinary" as ordinary and as something to be taken for granted.

This brings us not only face-to-face with, but already stumbling into the middle of, what I now regard as the central problem for theology today, a problem so subtle and complex, so little examined, yet so important, that I dare do no more at this point than call attention to it, acknowledge that I am not even beginning to do it justice, and then return to the discussion with the reservation that what follows must be placed in parentheses, subject to possible major revisions or even rejection when this foundation has been given its due attention. The problem which I have in mind is that of sorting out the ways in which we do justify for ourselves and to each other our ways of seeing, our perspectives, our (to give them a more honorific title) metaphysical beliefs.

Surely we do not want to say that just every "seeing as" "goes," that since everyone has some perspective, anyone may have whatever perspective he wants. We have a great deal to learn about just how we live our pluralism and relativism today, for although we must admit that it is a contradiction in terms to speak of an absolute relativism or an ultimate pluralism, we find that in our lives we do draw lines. Hitler's way of seeing and the presumed perspective of Lee Harvey Oswald are cases of "seeing as" which most of us condemn. It is all very well to say, as I did above, that "depending on our purposes, what we wish to accomplish, the context, and many other factors, we shall have what we call grounds for seeing a situation in one way rather than in another," but to what extent is this the case? How often can we give an account of our grounds, and how often can we sort out the "factors" which lead us to call our grounds good? Only in some cases (e.g., that of Hitler?) is it reasonably clear to us why we say that one perspective is to be preferred to another. When one rehearses the "factors" employed in making that "choice" (the one about Hitler), it seems clear that many if not all of them are inoperative in the "choice" between theological perspectives or between any one theological perspective and some so-called humanistic position.

I said that "we have grounds" for seeing things as we do. Let me confess that I am not at all clear about just what that means and that I am unable to give an account of this claim or its supports. If what follows stands no more in need of justification than other ways of seeing the business of theology, it is also no less in need of a justification. But what bothers me much more than this is that I am not at all sure I know what we are asking for if we ask for a justification for our ways of seeing. That said, I shall pursue, parenthetically, the contrasting proposals of seeing religion as grounded in a sense of limitation and as grounded in a sense of wonder.

Gordon Kaufman has more of the history of Christianity on the side of his proposed duality than I can claim. That says something about the influence of Augustine and Neo-Platonism on the history of Christianity. The idea of a Limit and man's limitedness fits well with a good deal of the traditional language of Christianity. On the other hand, I am inclined to judge that at least a good bit of the Old Testament, some of the New Testament and parts of the Christian tradition fit more smoothly into the duality of ordinary and extraordinary. The big advantage of Kaufman's proposal is that he can deal rather directly with the word "God." I am forced to shuffle around evasively, for I do not see a clear connection between a sense of the ordinary as extraordinary and speaking of the gods. I could say—which would probably be counted against me in our pro-Hebrew and anti-Greek theology of today—that I believe this is exactly what accounts for language about the gods in the Greek tragedians. But if I am going to win any points for my proposal in the contemporary discussions, I had better try another tack. Let me see what I can do with the parables of Jesus, for it is in puzzling over the reputed language of Jesus that I have come to wonder about the connections between the Bible and much of our Western theological tradition. Indeed, it is the way in which language about God occurs in the sayings of Jesus that leads me to wonder if transcendence is the word we want when thinking about the word "God." My proposed duality of extraordinary and ordinary is not made clearer by bringing in the idea of transcendence. One could say, I suppose, that if a man sees a situation which to the masses is very ordinary, but which strikes him as extraordinary precisely in its ordinariness, then the situation for him transcends ordinariness. I do not object to this way of speaking, but it seems a bit forced. It would seem clearer to say that he finds it amazing that the situation is as it is, that he sees it as wonderful, an occasion for rejoicing, perhaps for trembling, as by no means something to be shrugged off and "taken for granted." Given a certain background, he might even "speak of God" in such a situation. Let me try out this approach to language about God against the reputed sayings of Jesus of Nazareth.[8]

It is certain that Jesus did speak of God or his Father, and the context for that speaking was as certainly the language and life of Israel, a people whose prophets and poets were convinced that their history had been touched, again and again, by what they called Yahweh. But what was this, that is, how can *we* speak of that by which those strange ones understood themselves to have been touched? It is puzzling enough to try to say how *they* spoke of that by which they understood their history to have been touched. Perhaps it is not too far wrong to say that their poets present this Yahweh as a great, mysterious, wonderful, but profoundly human figure, but then we must add at once, human in just those ways in which Israel lived its own particular humanity: in passion, concreteness, imagination, and sensitivity. Yahweh was a powerfully Jewish figure, who thundered like an Amos, agonized like a Jeremiah, and loved like a Hosea. By what were they touched? By themselves? By their own strange, creative imagination, by their own wild dreams? How shall we understand their language who are so far removed from their way of life?

In any case, the prophet from Nazareth, whom later

Greeks called Jesus, added very little that was new, except for one thing: the warning or the promise, depending on how you take it, that whatever Yahweh was about, it was about right now, that the time was ripe, always ripe, that whatever Israel's dream meant, it meant it right now, not tomorrow.

This leaves unspecified what the content of that dream was, the dream which the prophet of Nazareth appears to have shared with the older prophets. What was God, or the Father, for Jesus? He was that which allows everything in this life to be just exactly as it is, the rain falling on the just as on the unjust. God is that which sees everything in our world just exactly as it happens: not a sparrow falls to the ground without notice. To speak of a world under God is to speak of the world seen openly and honestly as it appears to the Jewish prophetic vision, with no pretense, no covering up what is there, no sentimental blindness to what lies before our eyes, and blessed, therefore, are those who have eyes that do see, for not many have.

Many of the parables of Jesus speak of the coming or beginning of the reign of God over the world; how will it be then, with the realization of God's full authority over this world? In that hour, we are told, it will be just as things are now: seed dropping by the wayside, and only some of it landing in good ground and bringing up a rich crop, people being invited to dinner and most not bothering to take what is presented, opportunities of life before us, which a few grasp and most ignore. And what did the teller of the parables have to say to all this, to the life which in fact we all lead? He had this to say, that this was all real, indeed the only reality there is, that the taking or ignoring of these opportunities are not trivia, not preliminary, not secondary, but final, that who we are in such situations is who we are for good. No ghosts, no supernatural warnings or beings, no souls rising from the dead, the parable of the rich man and Lazarus tells us, will or can come to prove this to us, but the message of the parables, the human words of an imaginative human dreamer, the sign of the preacher Jonah, is all we have. And his word is this: our human life cannot be put in parentheses as preliminary, tentative, only a dress rehearsal for a later supposedly really real performance which is supposed to transcend it. To be ready for the kingdom means to start living now, in the present.

These parables are language, and to attend to them, Wittgenstein reminds us, is to attend to a form of life. Other forms of life, evidently enough, are also lived in our world, but this is one option. And what is the form of life presented there? Well, it is sort of like . . . and then follow the parables, little word-pictures of things as they are in our world, from time to time, of a man sowing his seed sloppily yet reaping a vast harvest, of a dinner party with guests who fail to show up and with others hurriedly invited at the last minute to replace the practical, cautious ones who were too busy to take time out for partying, of a man who wastes his inheritance and has the simplicity to return to his home and discovers that it is again his home. These stories are drawn from ordinary human life and do not pretend to speak of anything which transcends or lies beyond our life. No divine interventions, no heavenly beings, no unconditioned entities appear in them. Certainly not every party, not every seedtime or harvest, not every loss of money or son is seen just as they are in these stories. But some situations can sometimes be seen this way. These are an extraordinary reading, if you will, of what are also ordinary situations. And in the background of each tale, there stands a vague, almost passive and somewhat shadowy figure, the king, the father, the householder, who is as it were a sign that things *can* be seen—not have to be, but sometimes at least *can* be seen—as they are in these stories. The actors in the parables, the ones who stand in the center are servants, sons, guests, travelers, stewards, the strange ones of this world who dare to take life offers, who have the mad imagination to see this world as really theirs to possess. They win the world and their place in it by simplicity (the workers in the vineyard, the prodigal son), by cheating (the unjust steward), and by stubbornness (the widow and the unjust judge), but they win it. Or sometimes they don't. And there we are left: he who has ears to hear this imaginative version of life, this extraordinary vision of the ordinary, let him hear.

In what I have said so far, I have not denied that the language of Jesus appears to be that of a man who was able to hypostatize and personify a guarantor of the extraordinariness of the ordinary occasions which life

presents us. Using the imaginative and poetic images of
Israel, and living in an age and place when most men
would have said that someone (variously conceived) was
up there watching us (in various ways and with various
consequences), the Jesus of the New Testament documents spoke of God as an intensely personal figure, the
sort of personal figure to whom one could speak in prayer.
There was, so to speak, someone there, for him and for his
imagination, on the other end of the line. How little he
had to say in the way of offering a doctrine of God I have
already indicated. The one who was there on the other
end of the line was for Jesus, evidently, the one whose
will is that we deal with life and see it as a series of
opportunities to serve, love, visit and clothe our neighbor.
The question which seemed to be central for the prophet
of Nazareth was the question of whether men obeyed this
will, which is to say whether they would open the eyes of
their imagination to see life in this way. Not many men of
his time, he seemed to have thought, would do so. We
may fairly assume that not many "modern" men will do
any better.

The task for "the new theology" is, formally speaking,
not so different from that of any older theology. It is the
endless task of translation, of appropriating for today and
in our own way the insights and wisdom of the past in
such a way as to throw light on our own deepest experiences. That does not mean necessarily a translation into
"terms fully comprehensible and significant to the most

'modern' of men," for not all that is "modern" can be normative for this work. It must, of course, be our own appropriation, and I would therefore agree with Gordon Kaufman that this means that a dualism of which one pole is said to lie utterly "beyond" the realm of human experience will probably not be helpful. It is our task, I agree, to work out our own appropriation, though with fear and trembling, in terms of that strange complex which we call human experience. A duality there will be in our results, but a duality within human experience itself.

I have suggested a duality of "seeing as," specifically the duality of seeing the ordinary as extraordinary, but this could be developed also as the duality of imagination and factuality, of dreams as over against common sense, of poetry *versus* prose, of insight as distinct from explanation. But will this lead us to a doctrine of God? If we are to work within the dualities of human experience, is not a *doctrine* of God specifically what must be given up for the time being? The word "God" is a problem for theology today because we modern theologians are all too modern, the author of *The Secular Meaning of the Gospel* included, and therefore too literal, too prosaic, too unimaginative. We are accepting too uncritically the culturally privileged status of the language of factuality, explanation and the ordinary, and as a result we judge that we are saying too little if we locate "God" within the metaphorical language of imagination and insight. With all or most of our chips on one way of seeing the world and ourselves, we miss the full complexity and ambiguity of every "seeing as." A doctrine of God for our time smacks too much of clarity, explanation, and precision and therefore is not our right until we win our way clear of the charges of having been too clear, having too neat explanations and of having been too precise about matters which have led men of other ages to tremble. Men have had difficulty speaking of God, I suggest, not because God was beyond this world and our experience, but precisely because they were speaking of this world of human experience, a world of experience in which at least the strange ones of this world have known at least some "ordinary" situations in such a way that words failed them. Until theology has learned just this sort of speechlessness, may the gods or God save us from another doctrine of God. That is what I mean by asking whether "transcendence" is the word we want.

N O T E S

1. "On the Meaning of 'God': Transcendence without Mythology," *The Harvard Theological Review*, Vol. 59, No. 2 (April, 1966), pp. 105-132.
2. *Ibid.*, p. 108 n.
3. *Ibid.*, p. 106.
4. *Ibid.*, p. 107.
5. *Ibid.*, p. 109.
6. *Tractatus*, 6.44.
7. *Op. cit.*, p. 114.
8. The dependence of the following on the writings of Werner and Lotte Pelz is gladly acknowledged. Cf. *God is No More, Distant Strains of Triumph*, and especially *True Deceivers*.